Werner and Susanne Lantermann

Cockatoos

Acclimation, Care, Feeding, Sickness, and Breeding
Special Chapter: Understanding Cockatoos

Consulting Editor: Matthew M. Vriends, PhD

With Color Photographs by Well-known Animal Photographers
and Drawings by Fritz W. Köhler

BARRON'S

All inquiries should be addressed to:
Barron's Educational Series, Inc.
250 Wireless Boulevard
Hauppauge, NY 11788

Library of Congress Catalog Card No.   89-6634

International Standard Book No. 0-8120-4159-3

Library of Congress Cataloging-in-Publication Data

Lantermann, Werner, 1956—
    [Kakadus. English]
    Cockatoos: acclimation, care, feeding, sickness,
and breeding: special chapter, Understanding
cockatoos/Werner and Susanne Lantermann:
consulting editor, Matthew M.Vriends; with color
photographs by animal photographers and drawings by
Fritz W. Kohler; [translated from the German by
Elizabeth D. Crawford].
    Translation of: Kakadus.
    Bibliography: p. 59
    Includes index.
    ISBN 0-8120-4159-3
    1. Cockatoos. Lantermann, Susanne. II Title.
SF473.C63L3513 1989
636.6'865—dc20   89-6634
                                   CIP

Printed in Hong Kong

6 7 8   4900   13 12 11

The color photographs on the covers show:
Front cover: Lesser sulphur-crested Cockatoo .
Inside front cover: Goffin's Cockatoo.
Inside back cover: Moluccan Cockatoo.
Back Cover: (above) Rose-breasted cockatoo; (below
left) Moluccan Cockatoo; (below right) Goffin's Cocka-
too.

Photo credits:
Lantermann: page 9; Martin: page 38 (above left and
below right); Pfeffer: page 38 (above right and below
left); Schweiger: pages 45 and 46; Skogstad: front cover;
inside front cover; pages 10, 27, 28 and 37; inside back
cover; and back cover.

About the authors:
Werner Lantermann has been director of a private
institute for parrot research in Oberhausen since 1981.
His specialty is the large parrots of South and Central
America. He is the author of numerous publications in
professional journals and successful books about parrot-
keeping and breeding, among them Barron's *The New
Parrot Handbook* and *Amazon Parrots*.

Susanne Lantermann is a co-worker in the private
institute for parrot research in Oberhausen and co-author
of numerous books about African and South American
parrots.

Note and warning
People who suffer from an allergy to feathers or feather
dust should not keep any kind of parrot. If you are in any
doubt, check with your doctor.

    You may receive bites or scratches in handling
parrots. Any such wounds should be treated by a doctor
immediately.

    Psittacosis (parrot fever) is not one of the common
parrot diseases (see page 31), but it can produce some
life-threatening symptoms of illness in people and to
some extent in parrots. Therefore: consult the doctor immediately if any symptoms of cold or flu appear (see
page 34).

Contents

Foreword

Cockatoo, a Malaysian word, has been said to mean "old Father" or "pincer"—the latter meaning being quite clear to anyone who has ever felt the sharp beak of a cockatoo. A neglected, poorly maintained cockatoo, which has neither human nor fellow bird for a constant companion, not only can develop into the proverbial "pincer," but into a pitiful feather plucker as well—a bird that eventually will sit in his cage completely featherless, with only the characteristic feather crest remaining to betray that he is a cockatoo. Yet, when properly kept and cared for, these sociable parrots are the most lovable creatures, whose endless inventiveness and extraordinary playfulness enchant an ever-increasing number of cockatoo fanciers.

This book answers all the important questions that can arise about the correct maintenance of cockatoos. Parrot experts Werner and Susanne Lantermann pass along their knowledge and experience, explaining why cockatoos are best kept in pairs, what you should take into consideration before buying a cockatoo, how a proper cockatoo cage should look, and what foods are suitable.

In the chapter "Health and Sickness," the authors give advice on how to avoid illness and what to do if the parrot does become sick. Because they know that many cockatoos are now threatened with extinction in their native habitat, the authors urge the cockatoo fancier to try to breed them and also provide detailed instructions. A special chapter is devoted to the eight cockatoo species now included under the jurisdiction of the species-protection regulations. The description includes detailed information on appearance, range, and habitat, and special advice for maintenance.

The chapter "Understanding Cockatoos," which describes the most important behavior patterns of these lively and playful parrots, will help you to understand and observe cockatoo habits.

This book shows the beginner the way to the proper keeping of cockatoos and also offers the experienced cockatoo owner new and useful suggestions.

The easy-to-follow advice and instructions are illustrated with numerous informative drawings and fascinating color photographs, some of them published here for the first time.

Authors and publisher thank all who have worked on this book: the animal photographers, especially Karin Skogstad, for the extraordinarily beautiful photographs, the artist Fritz W. Köhler for the informative drawings, and the veterinarian Dr. Gabriele Wiesner for checking the chapter "Health and Illness."

Considerations Before Buying

How Cockatoos Differ from Other Parrots

Cockatoos are different from other parrots in looks as well as in behavior:

Plumage: Their single-colored plumage, usually white or dark, and their mobile crest of feathers are in contrast to the brightly colored plumage of Aras or Amazons.

Devotion: More than any other parrots, cockatoos that are brought into a household as young birds and become attached to an individual will in time become so devoted and tame that separation becomes almost impossible without injury to the cockatoo. That special person must pay a great deal of attention to the cockatoo every day. This requires committing much time to filling the more or less involuntary role of a partner.

Such birds will get used to a mate only with the greatest difficulty and are therefore hard to use for attempts at breeding. Scarcely any cockatoo-keeper is aware of this consequence when beginning attempts at taming.

Playfulness and Loud Cries: Almost all cockatoo species demonstrate extraordinary playfulness, with a wealth of endless inventiveness. Tame house birds all learn some tricks, shaking and climbing exercises, or the use of various objects as "tools." Such activities are carried out all day long without interruption, except for brief rest periods, so that the birds are almost constantly in motion. Cockatoos accompany their play with loud cries, which in the large species can sometimes escalate to a deafening, prolonged shriek.

Beak Strength: The enormous power of the beak of some cockatoos should not go unmentioned. Scarcely any other of the large parrot species can do so much with its beak as the cockatoo. With ease it demolishes objects such as ordinary plastic food dishes, for example, not to mention the whittling away of perches. The larger cockatoos are also able to bend the bars of the ordinary parrot cage in a very short time and crack the solder joints.

Mutual preening: Two cockatoos who get along well together preen each other's plumage, especially in the places the birds can't reach by themselves.

Therefore additional security is advised for cage doors (see page 13). Buying a suitable, stable (and therefore, unfortunately, expensive) cage is a prerequisite for keeping cockatoos.

Ability to Imitate: You shouldn't have any great expectations about the ability of cockatoos to "talk." There are individual birds who, after systematic training, can repeat some human words, the sounds of animals, or household sounds. These "speech artists" are usually found among the African gray parrots and Amazons. Cockatoos are more likely to imitate movement. Many performers utilize this characteristic when they teach their cockatoos to "dance," roller skate, or play tug of war.

Considerations Before Buying a Single Bird

When you've become somewhat familiar with the cockatoo's "character traits" and decide that keep-

Considerations Before Buying

The characteristic feathered crests of the cockatoos are very different in form. They are termed pointed (foreground) and rounded (rear right and left)).

ing one might be possible, you need to think carefully about the following points:

Cockatoos without partners require the constant attention of the keeper. The ever more intense animal-human relationship generates a time-consuming responsibility that is scarcely predictable at the beginning, which some people are not able to handle over the long term.

For feeding a single cockatoo, you should plan an average of 20 to 30 minutes of working time per day. This involves preparing the food, cleaning the feed dishes and the cage surroundings inside the house, as well as daily dusting, for cockatoos regularly produce feather dust (see page 21).

The loud voice of a cockatoo can lead to difficulties, especially if you live in an apartment house. Find out ahead of time if your landlord and neighbors will tolerate a parrot being kept nearby.

During vacation and in case you are ill, the cockatoo should be cared for by someone it already knows. Plan ahead for this.

The cost of buying a cockatoo and the proper equipment for keeping one is quite expensive.

Considerations Before Buying a Pair

Basically the considerations already mentioned apply to buying a pair of cockatoos. In addition:

Two cockatoos who get along well together make fewer demands on the keeper's time because they are not so dependent as a single bird on his or her constant attention.

The burden of noise will naturally be much greater when you have more than one bird. Especially when you are keeping cockatoos in an outdoor aviary, their cries can lead to trouble with noise-sensitive neighbors.

The daily time needed for cleaning and care increases. The time expenditure for preparing food can be even greater if you want to breed cockatoos (see page 35).

Keeping more than two cockatoos is especially interesting for the cockatoo fancier who has breeding in mind. In this case, the construction of a bird room (see page 14) or building an aviary and bird shelter (page 15) is recommended.

Cockatoos and Other Parrots

Other Parrots of the Same Size: Cockatoos usually get along fairly well with other parrots of the same size if there are enough opportunities for freedom of movement inside the cage or aviary. However, you should never add a third bird to an already established pair of cockatoos. It would most likely be harried by the "master of the house," chased, and sooner or later would have to be separated from the pair.

Smaller Parrakeets and Parrot Species: We do not consider a combination advisable. The smaller psittacines are apt to quickly fall prey to the strong beak of the cockatoo. Exceptions prove the rule!

Cockatoos and Other Pets

Dogs and Cats: In some cases cockatoos can get along well with these other pets, if both parties are allowed gradually to get used to each other. Cats, for example, after one uncomfortable encounter with the strong cockatoo beak, often make a wide circuit around a parrot cage. Albeit, harmonious relationships among dogs, cats, and large parrots are occasionally cited in newspapers. You have to try to see what works and what doesn't in your own situation.

Small Pets: Direct contact with cockatoos frequently ends in fatality for small mammals like guinea pigs, hamsters, or mice. Smaller birds like zebra finches or canaries will also quickly fall prey to the cockatoo.

Cockatoos and Children

Babies and small children must never be left alone with a cockatoo that has the freedom of the house. If a baby competes for what was once the cockatoo's position as favorite, the bird may react

This cockatoo uses a short branch to help scratch. The use of "tools" to help perform tasks is a sign of cockatoos' intelligence.

with jealousy, attacking the child with its beak or sharp claws.

Older children and teenagers, however, can gradually become familiar with the habits of a cockatoo. At the same time they also learn how to assume responsibility for a caged bird, which requires regular care and feeding and must never be neglected.

Advice for Buying a Bird

Where You Can Buy Cockatoos

Pet Shop: If you are a first-time parrot-keeper, it's a good idea to get your cockatoo in a well-managed pet shop or in the pet department of one of the larger department stores. Most of the cockatoos sold there have been caught in the wild, although some pet dealers also do try to handle birds bred in captivity. Thus, before each cockatoo finds a buyer, several weeks have passed during which the imported bird has grown somewhat used to living in a cage and has adapted to commercial feed.

Direct Importers and Wholesalers: In certain instances cockatoos will be sold to private individuals. However, only an experienced parrot-keeper should acquire a cockatoo in this way.

Breeders: For some time, young cockatoos of the umbrella-crested, lesser sulphur-crested, greater sulphur-crested, and rose-breasted cockatoo species bred in this country, as well as in Europe, have been available. These cockatoos are already well adapted to climate and feeding conditions, are disease-resistant, and, in addition, are cage- or even hand-tame. However, the opportunities to procure such a young bird are still rather limited at the moment. Many breeders often ask extraordinarily high prices for their birds.

Newspaper Advertisements: Private cockatoo-keepers sometimes offer their extra birds in the professional publications (see page 59).

Zoos or Bird Sanctuaries: Sometimes it's worth an inquiry, for often "discarded" cockatoos end up there. However, much patience and love is required to get such a bird used to a new primary person or able to be used for breeding.

Choosing a Healthy Cockatoo

Proper evaluation of a cockatoo's health status is not very easy for a layperson. However, the following checklist may help you to be halfway certain:

Housing: Cages and aviaries with thick layers of droppings, dirty interior fittings, and feeding dishes containing only one type of grain and dirty drinking water, possibly are evidence of poor bird care. This may affect the health of the cockatoos.

Appearance of the Cockatoos: The plumage should lie smooth and be intact. It is not advisable to buy a cockatoo with plumage that is lusterless, appears ruffled, or has bare spots.

The nostrils and the area around the nose should be dry and clear.

The eyes should be round (not slitted), clear, shining, and not sticky.

Generally a sick cockatoo has an apathetic, distressed appearance. It sleeps a great deal, rests on both legs—in contrast to a healthy (adult) bird—(see page 21), and takes little or no nourishment.

Missing claws or missing toes are beauty flaws, not signs of illness, which occur mainly through bites from other birds. Sometimes such cockatoos are sold at a reduced price. Nevertheless, birds intended for breeding should display a complete set of claws.

Droppings: The droppings of a healthy bird consist of an olive green and white urea portion, and should be medium firm and formed. Unformed, watery, different-colored, or even bloody stool can be an indication of serious illness, but sometimes diarrhea can be caused by psychosomatic factors.

Behavior: During the brief buying encounter, it's hardly possible to tell whether a cockatoo is showing behavioral disturbances, so general rules can't be established. The most conspicuous disturbances are compulsive (stereotypical) movements, that is, motions that are constantly repeated. Neu-

Greater sulphur-crested cockatoo.
Millet spray is a favorite parrot treat.

rotic screaming and feather plucking (see page 33), which usually begins on the back and abdominal areas, are also behavioral disturbances that should always cause you to reconsider your intention to buy.

Note: Besides feather plucking, there is a plumage disease, psittacine beak and feather syndrome (see Signs of Illness, page 34). So far it has been identified in the so-called white cockatoos, and especially in the Moluccans, but it is certain that it also occurs in African gray parrots, cockatiels, and other species. Ailing birds often die within a few months. Buying such a bird is of course extremely inadvisable.

Determining Sex

In the majority of cockatoo species, the sex is easy to determine. Of the species discussed in this book, the females of the lesser sulphur-crested, greater sulphur-crested, umbrella-crested, Goffin's, rose-breasted, and Philippine cockatoo display a brown, chestnut-brown, or red-brown iris color. The iris of the male cockatoo of these species is dark brown to black. Basically this also applies to the Moluccan cockatoo, except that the iris of the female is dark brown and is not so easy to diffferentiate from the color of the male iris in ordinary daylight. With a small pocket flashlight, however, you can briefly illuminate the bird in question and can as a rule determine the sex accurately. In the bare-eyed cockatoo, both sexes have a dark iris. The differences in this species lie in the body size (male is larger) and a less extensive unfeathered area around the eye of the female. With this species (sometimes with the Moluccan cockatoo, too) you can be absolutely certain only with an endoscopic examination, which can be carried out at a quite reasonable cost at many veterinary colleges and by qualified veterinarians.

Determining Age

Cockatoos are said to be the longest lived of any of the parrots. Cases have been cited of greater sulphur-crested cockatoos with good care living to be one hundred years old. Very often, particularly when breeding is attempted, it is necessary to know the age of the bird. Aside from captive-bred young birds, whose ages usually are known exactly, the ages of imported cockatoos cannot be determined without further testing. But there are some indications by which young and old birds can usually be distinguished.

The plumage of the old bird has all the typical markings (see species descriptions, page 45). In young birds, the yellow cheek patch, for example, or the yellow crest color (in lesser and greater sulphur-crested cockatoos) is paler. The plumage of young rose-breasted cockatoos is duller all over. Young greater sulphur-crested cockatoos and umbrella-crested cockatoos often show pale gray shadows in the plumage. In young Philippine cockatoos the tail feathers are salmon-colored and become red only with age.

The iris color undergoes a color change over the course of several months and years. In adult female cockatoos, the iris is usually intense red or red-brown in color, whereas in birds under two years old, as a rule, it is dark brown or yellow-brown.

The beak of a young bird is shiny and smooth, and without the visible stratifications that develop with the growth of horn in older parrots.

The feet of younger cockatoos display a somewhat more widely spread scale structure.

In the first weeks of life, young birds rest on both

Goffin's cockatoos.
The female attentively watches her partner preening (left) and stretches her head forward (right), inviting him to preen it; however her partner reacts differently from the way she expected (below).

feet after flying and only later adopt the typical one-legged sleeping and resting position.

Formalities of Purchase

When buying a cockatoo, there are various legal regulations that must be observed. The overall guiding principle is the Washington agreement, the Convention on International Trade in Endangered Species (CITES) of Wild Flora and Fauna (hereafter referred to as WA), which comprehensively lists all animal and plant species that are threatened, endangered, or threatened with extinction. (See page 54.) The agreement is divided into three categories (Appendices I through III). All cockatoo species (with the exception of the palm cockatoo, which is listed in Appendix I and is one of the animal species threatened with extinction) are entered in Appendix II of the WA, which lists those species that are under special regulation but that may still be bought and sold. According to the WA and to the European and American legal regulations, for their import, an export license from the country of origin and an import license from the country of import are required. The cockatoos offered by reputable pet dealers meet these criteria and can be purchased without concern if the buyer receives certain certificates with the animal.

CITES Certificate: This certificate, which can be displayed as the bird's "passport," confirms to the receiver that the .animal has been imported properly in compliance with the requirements of the WA or was bred in compliance with regulations in Europe. European bred birds may be sold only after the second generation and even then only with special permission to be excepted from the Endangered Species Regulation.

Leg Band or Ring: Make sure at the time of purchase that the bird is wearing an official leg band or ring and that the number of this ring is identical with the number on the CITES certificate.

Sales Contract: In every well-managed animal dealership, it is a matter of course for the buyer to be given a detailed sales agreement. Dealerships in Germany, for example, belonging to the Central Committee of Animal Dealers, have prepared a so-called "Pet Pass"—an excellent agreement that other countries should follow! This agreement lists: Date of sale, bird species as well as subspecies, leg ring number, CITES certificate number, sale price, addresses of seller and buyer. Also, the sex of the bird should be noted, if the seller has undertaken determination of the sex and it is a decisive consideration for the buyer. Concrete written agreements like this sales contract are also advisable for exchanges, loans, breeding cooperatives, or presents.

Duty to Report: In various European countries, four weeks at the latest after acquiring the animal, the new owner must report the possession to the appropriate conservation office (as a rule it is the superior or the inferior conservation office). The new owners can get reporting forms from the pet dealer if he belongs to the Central Committee of Animal Dealers. The following information is required: Species of bird, age, sex, origin, domicile, permanent residence, intended purpose, and leg band number.

Housing and Equipment

Keeping a Cockatoo Indoors

The Indoor Cage

For the most part, it's the smaller cockatoo species (see descriptions of species, page 45) that can be kept, as single birds, in a large, stable, commercially available parrot cage.

Cage Size: For a single bird or for temporary accommodation of a pair, the cage must have a floor surface area of at least 27 × 27 inches (70 × 70 cm) and a height of 39 inches (100 cm). Models suitable for cockatoos are usually available in pet stores and the pet departments of large department stores.

Cage Shape: A parrot cage should be square, with a right-angled base; round cages are unsuitable.

Cage Grill: The cage bars must be horizontal so that the cockatoo can climb and the gauge should be heavy enough so that the bird can't bend the grill with its strong beak.

Droppings Tray: Commercially available parrot cages have trays for catching droppings that can be pulled out like a drawer. For the smaller cockatoo species, plastic trays are perfectly suitable. Larger species (see description of species, page 45) will quickly gnaw the plastic droppings trays to pieces, so you're better off with galvanized steel.

Cage Door: The cage door should be large enough so that the parrot can climb in and out without any difficulty. Some cockatoos learn very quickly how to open the cage door with their beaks, so it is advisable to secure the door with a snap hook.

The Indoor Aviary

Preparation of an indoor aviary is essential for permanent caging of a pair of cockatoos, as it is for housing a single bird of the larger cockatoo species (see description of species, page 45). The so-called modular cages, which are constructed of separate individual elements, are the best for this purpose.

The floor area of an aviary should be a mini-

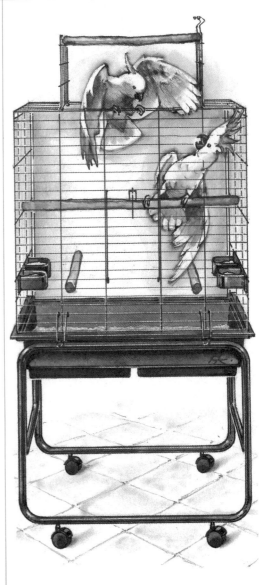

Parrot cage with outside perch:
You can keep two of the smaller cockatoo species in a cage like this if they are allowed to fly every day.

13

Housing and Equipment

mum of 39 × 39 inches (100 × 100 cm), the height about 78 inches (200 cm). An appropriate indoor aviary can be constructed from four aviary elements of 39 × 78 inches (100 × 200 cm) and a roof element of 39 × 39 inches (100 × 100 cm). This aviary can be expanded as necessary or divided by slide-in partitions. This arrangement is also suitable if you want to try breeding the smaller cockatoo species.

Mesh size, wire gauge, back walls, and equipment for the aviaries are available in different styles. Look at manufacturers' catalogs in the pet shop or the pet department of a large department store and get advice on which aviary is suitable for your particular purpose.

The Bird Room

A bird room is almost the ideal setup for keeping cockatoos. For this you need an empty room, with windows, in which the cockatoos can move freely without any cage boundaries.

However, such a room needs careful preparation to make it suitable for cockatoos:

• All carpets, wall, and ceiling coverings must be removed.
• Walls and ceiling must be covered with a nontoxic coat of whitewash or latex paint (available from a paint dealer), or be tiled.
• Doors, heating units, exposed electrical wires, electrical outlets, light switches, and light fixtures should be covered with tin or wire mesh.
• It's a good idea to seal the floor so that no dampness can get through to rooms underneath.
• Wooden floors or carpeted floors should be converted to ceramic tiles.
• The amount of equipment needed depends on the number of birds: climbing trees (see page 16), bathing pans, a feeding board with removable dishes, and nest boxes (page 15).

Compared with an outdoor aviary (see page 16), keeping parrots in a bird room has certain distinct advantages:

• The cockatoos live in a controlled, evenly maintained climate.
• The loud voices of the cockatoos are not so audible to neighbors living nearby.
• There is less danger of theft.
  Disadvantages include:
• The parrots receive only a limited amount of daylight.
• There is no chance for them to get direct sunshine.
• The cockatoos' plumage never receives the benefit of a natural rain shower in cleaning off feather dust.

Equipment for Cages and Aviaries

Perches: Use round perches with a diameter of about 1 inch (25–30 mm) for smaller cockatoos (see description of species, page 45); for larger species the diameter should be 1½ to 2 inches (35–45 mm). It's good to have the perches of varying thicknesses so that the birds' feet don't go lame. The branches of unsprayed fruit trees (after being carefully scrubbed under hot running water) have proven to be excellent. Their rough upper surfaces are good for wearing down the claws of the cockatoos by natural means, as well as for "foot exercises." The perches need to be mounted in the cage in such a way that the bowls for water and food will not be fouled by the falling droppings of the birds.

Depending on the size of the cage or the bird room, you should provide the cockatoos with the opportunity to use their wings. Place two perches in the upper area, as far as possible from each other, and don't obstruct the "runway" with climbing or chewing equipment.

Food and Drinking Dishes: When you buy a parrot cage, ordinary plastic food and drinking bowls are usually included in the price. Plastic dishes will be gnawed to pieces by the cockatoos in a short time and must then be changed. Better food and water dishes are those made of pottery or stainless steel, which can be fastened in the cage, aviary, or bird room with special holders (all available from the pet dealer). (There should be a total of four, see page 29).

Exercise equipment like large-link chains, climbing ropes, or fresh branches for gnawing are important for the caged cockatoo.

Bathing Pans: Cockatoos like to bathe to get rid of feather dust. Shallow clay flowerpot saucers with a diameter of 12 to 14 inches (30–35 cm) are excellent for this purpose. The birdbath is placed on the floor of the cage or fastened in an aviary with a special holder (available from the pet dealer) about 39 inches (1 m) above the floor.

Play and Exercise Equipment: Chains with large links, climbing ropes, fresh branches for gnawing, and wooden parrot toys (pet dealer) present the single bird as well as aviary birds with opportunities to exercise and provide variety in their caged existence; they also serve to maintain the health of beak and claws.

Caution: Do not use any branches from poisonous trees or shrubs! For example, acacia, yew, laburnum, viburnum, black honeysuckle, holly, dwarf elder, and many evergreens are all poisonous (see Useful Literature and Addresses, page 59).

Limestone: It's pointless to put a limestone block into a cockatoo cage. The cockatoo will peck

it to pieces within minutes and throw it on the floor. The remains are then ignored completely. Minerals must be added to the food in powdered form (see Vitamins and Minerals, pages 26-29).

Litter: The floor of the cage or aviary should be strewn with sand (see Vitamins and Minerals, pages 26-29). Use either clean river sand or the special bird sand from the pet shop. Bird sand often contains an anise additive, which diminishes the odor of the bird cage.

Nest Boxes: If you want to breed parrots, you should make arrangements ahead of time so that you can introduce a nest box (see Prerequisites for Successful Breeding, page 35) into an aviary or a bird room and be able to check it.

Placement of Cage or Aviary: Choose a quiet corner of the living room that is bright, airy, draft-free, and usually sunny. The cage or the aviary should be placed here permanently. A single bird's cage must be placed in a frequently used room, so that the cockatoo can take part in the life of the family and will not become bored. Never put the cage directly on the floor. This makes the cockatoo feel insecure. A somewhat elevated location (about eye level) is preferable, so that the cockatoo can look out over its surroundings.

Free Flight in the House

Freedom to fly about the house is particularly important for the cockatoo. It provides the bird with the necessary change from its dreary cage life and offers it the chance to get enough exercise. After the bird is acclimated (see page 18), open the cage door to the cockatoo and, an hour at a time, get it used to staying outside the cage. However, never let the bird fly around the house unsupervised. It can get hurt (see Table of Dangers, page 23) or sometimes do terrible damage to the house and furniture.

Caution: Remove all houseplants so that the cockatoo can't nibble or eat them. Otherwise poisoning and death might result!

Housing and Equipment

Free Perch and Climbing Tree Indoors

Under supervision, hand-tame cockatoos can be kept during the day for hours at a time on a free perch or climbing tree. It's a pleasant change for the cockatoo, and the keeper can then enjoy watching the acrobatic skills of his bird. The parrot should spend the rest of the time in its cage and it should be fed there. In time, the bird develops a regular daily rhythm. Eventually it will return voluntarily to its cage with hunger and the onset of darkness. Cockatoos that have such closely cut pinions (see page 21) that they are unable to fly back into their cage and need a climbing aid, such as a long, firmly fastened branch reaching from climbing tree to cage.

Free Perch: The simplest form of free perch indoors is one that is fastened onto the roof of the cage with a bracket. It should be mounted approxi-mately 6 inches (15 cm) above the roof and not extend to the side beyond the cage measurements, so that the bird droppings will fall into the cage and not onto the living room floor. The opportunities for the cockatoo to exercise on such a perch are quite limited, however.

Climbing Tree: For a climbing tree you need a flowerpot filled with sand or a cement pot (diameter about 39 inches [100 cm]; height about 7½ inches [50 cm]) and a well-branched limb. To keep the branch upright in the container, dampen the sand somewhat before you put it in the container and then tamp it down well. Of course you can also get suitable climbing trees in the pet store. The more chances to climb the "tree" offers, the better for the cockatoo.

Warning: Improperly fastened perches or ones that break suddenly can injure the bird or even kill it with a fall.

This climbing tree, firmly fastened in a cement pot filled with sand, consists of a well-branched natural limb to which perches have been added.

Keeping Cockatoos Outdoors

A bird shelter with a garden flight cage attached offers the cockatoos the best possible quality of life they can enjoy in human captivity.

The parrots have light, air, sun, rain, and opportunities to dig, fly, or climb. If you plan to try to breed and to keep several cockatoos, this form of housing or a bird room is highly recommended. Precise instructions for the construction of such an aviary sometimes appear in the periodical literature (see page 59).

Tips for Building the Bird Shelter

Your building plans must allow for several basic considerations:

• Find out about local building regulations and whether a building permit is necessary.

Housing and Equipment

• Use only very strong construction materials, ones that can stand up under the strong beaks of the cockatoos.
• The bird shelter should be built of brick or stone and sit on a solid cement foundation. Good insulation saves on heating.
• The use of simple transparent glass bricks for windows is recommended.
• The fly-through to the flight cage is created with a glass-brick-equipped aluminum swivel window (size about 19½ × 9³/₄ inches (50 × 25 cm).
• Ceramic tiles are particularly good for covering the walls and floor because they are easy to clean.
• Heating, light (fluorescents), and running water are essential features for the bird shelter.
• The size of the inside space: a floor surface of 78 × 39 inches (2 × 1 m) and 78 inches (2 m) in height is enough for a pair of cockatoos.
• The equipment for the interior consists of a feeding board with removable dishes, several perches, and a nest box.

   Note: Besides conforming to code requirements, the proposed aviary and bird shelter should be approved as to their suitability for proper maintenance of the birds.

The Flight Cage

   The flight cage should be attached to the shelter so that the cockatoos can leave their inner room even in bad weather. The following points must be when you are building the flight cage:

• For a pair of the smaller species (see description of species, page 45) a flight of 78 to 117 inches (2–3 m) in length and 78 inches (2 m) in height is enough. For the larger species you need a larger flight.
• It is advisable to lay a cement foundation (being careful to observe building codes).
• Ready-made aviary elements (see the Indoor Aviary, page 13) can be mounted directly on the footing.
• If you are handy with tools you can make the cage supports yourself from galvanized steel pipes (bolted or welded).
• It's best to use galvanized rectangular wire mesh for fencing. Mesh size of 0.8 × 0.8 inches (19 × 19 mm) and wire gauge of 0.04 to 0.06 inches (1.05–1.50 mm) will do for small cockatoos; for larger birds use mesh size of 2 × 2 inches (50 × 50 mm) and wire gauge of 0.16 inches (4 mm).
• Rats, mice, and other small mammals carry disease or even kill cockatoos if they get into the aviary. Therefore be sure to secure the large-meshed fencing from the outside with a fence of smaller mesh size.
• A third of the flight should be roofed over to offer the cockatoos shelter from too much rain or sun.
• Paving flags are especially good for the flight cage floor. Many cockatoos like to scratch and dig in the ground; you can add a thick layer of dirt or sand.
• For the entrance to the flight cage, it is recommended to make a small outer door that is secured with a space and a second door, like an air lock, to keep the cockatoos from escaping.
• The equipment for the aviary consists of climbing trees, baths, and several perches (see page 14).

Acclimation And Care

Taking Your Bird Home

After you've bought your cockatoo, you should transport it home as quickly as possible. During a longer trip by car, it is important to place the cockatoo in a special animal carrier, which should be equipped with a food dish and a perch. The cage should be just large enough so that the cockatoo can turn around and can sit upright in it.

Transporting in a parrot cage is advisable only with tame birds and for short car trips. Untamed cockatoos will flutter wildly in such cages and injure themselves.

Acclimation

A fully-equipped cage—away from other parrots and house pets—should be awaiting the cockatoo upon its arrival in its new home. The parrot will only cautiously leave the transport carrier and will examine its new cage before entering it.

The cockatoo will take between four and six weeks to become accustomed to its new surroundings. During this period you should:

Stretching movements, such as slight lifting and spreading of the wings over the back, can often be observed after rest periods.

• Provide the cockatoo with peace and give it time to learn to know its new environment.
• Keep visitors and resident pets well away from it.
• Confine your maintenance jobs to providing food and water and perform only the essential cleaning operations.
• Do not let it out of the cage.
• In the beginning keep the room temperature constant at about 72°F (22°C).

During the acclimation period you can:
• Slowly accustom the cockatoo to a balanced, varied diet (see Correct Feeding, page 29).
• Obtain a fecal sample (leave a sheet of plastic on the bottom of the cage) and take it to the veterinarian for examination.
• Decrease the maintenance temperature bit by bit, if the cockatoo is intended for the aviary.
• Undertake the first steps in taming (see page 19).

Before you put the cockatoo in with other parrots and transfer it to the aviary or bird room, you must:
• Get the cockatoo used to its food.
• Accustom the bird to the lower maintenance temperature.
• Be sure its droppings are free of infectious agents (get two fecal examinations from the veterinarian, fourteen days apart).
• Be sure the parrot is in good general condition. Its behavior should be lively and it should exhibit no abnormalities (see Choosing a Healthy Cockatoo, page 8).

Placement in an Aviary

A cockatoo that is intended for an aviary is always first introduced into the bird shelter. If possible, first place the parrot in a separate section inside the shelter so that it can get comfortable with its new surroundings. With a freshly imported cockatoo, particularly, great care must be taken to integrate the bird into the already established aviary community. The temperature in the shelter should not be substantially lower than the temperature maintained during the weeks of acclimation (see page 18). The connecting hatch to the flight cage should not be opened until a cockatoo has become familiar with the dimensions of the bird shelter, finds the perches without great difficulty, and regularly visits the feeding dish.

Some birds must be placed in the flight cage and brought back into the shelter again before they learn to find the way by themselves.

Note: Freshly imported cockatoos should be put in the aviary in early summer and can be kept there until late fall. Such parrots pass the winter in the bird house at temperatures of 46° to 50°F (8°–0°C).

Handling a Single Bird

Intensive contact with its keeper is extremely important for the single bird, because the cockatoo has a great need for social contact, i.e., for a partner. With the onset of sexual maturity this need becomes even stronger. Then the lack of a sexual partner can send the cockatoo into an emotional decline. Some birds respond by beginning to scream, pulling out their feathers, or becoming neurotically compulsive. It's high time for you to begin to think about getting a second cockatoo (see page 20).

Cage-taming

Cage-tame describes a cockatoo that allows you to approach without its jumping from the perch in alarm and retreating into a corner of its cage. Although a single bird later binds very closely to the keeper as a substitute for a missing social partner, it vigorously resists human influence at the beginning. The cockatoo screams, retreats, and bites if the keeper's hand comes near it. However, eventually patience, soothing words, and gentle movements will allay the parrot's natural anxiety.

Hand-taming

Hand-tame describes a parrot that willingly climbs onto your hand and allows itself to be carried around the house. To achieve this requires some patience. Avoiding abrupt movement, repeatedly offer the cockatoo treats, such as peanuts or pieces of apple, on your hand from outside through the cage wire. Eventually the parrot will carefully run up to your hand and take the piece of food. Next, open the cage door and hold a piece of food inside

Courtship behavior. The male draws attention to himself by fanning his tail, ruffling his feathers, spreading his wings, and erecting his crest.

the cage. If the cockatoo has learned to feel that your hand offers no threat, it won't be long before it allows itself to be scratched and climbs onto your hand.

"Learning to Speak"

Speaking, or more correctly, the imitation of human words is, for parrots, a form of making contact with their caretakers. All large parrots possess the ability (some more, some less) to imitate words or various sounds. In general, cockatoos do

Acclimation And Care

Synchronous stretching. Firmly bonded cockatoos often carry out synchronous movements, like these rose-breasted cockatoos stretching the same wing and fanning their tails.

not master this skill to a high degree, but through patient schooling eventually you can succeed in training any cockatoo to produce one or another word or short phrases. Vowels (a,e,i,o,u) usually can be imitated better than consonants or sibilants.

If You Keep Two Cockatoos Indoors

Without question, keeping a pair of cockatoos is better than keeping just one. Usually a cockatoo owner already has one bird before deciding to get a second. Of course it isn't entirely easy to bring two strange parrots together. Be sure to choose a bird of the opposite sex (see Determining Sex, page 11) of the same cockatoo species or subspecies—do not get just any cockatoo or a different species of parrot. Many times you may thus get a harmonious pair that may even breed in the right circumstances.

Getting Used to Each Other: Never put two strange birds together right off. First the cockatoos should observe and get to know each other—separated by a cage wall—for several days or weeks. Only then do you bring both parrots together on "neutral ground," that is, not in the cage of the "master of the house," and observe their behavior. The mood of the cockatoos is easy to determine by the fanning of the tail or the erection of the crest (see Courtship Behavior, page 36). If the meeting continues without any disturbances, they may remain together in the same cage; otherwise they should be separated and the attempt repeated until both birds come to an agreement.

Note: A single bird loses a little of its original tameness as it turns more to its mate than to its caretaker. The newly acquired cockatoo, on the other hand, quickly loses its shyness and imitates the already tamed partner in dealing with humans. It will become cage-tame in a shorter time, even hand-tame in the right circumstances. Pairs that get along well together can often be left completely alone, for they can keep each other occupied.

Care Measures for House Birds

Showering: If the cockatoo has no bathing dish in its cage, it must be showered weekly so that it can get rid of its feather dust. Smaller cages—without the droppings tray—may be placed bird and all in the bathtub and showered with a gentle spray of lukewarm water. Recently acquired birds should become accustomed to the shower slowly. Leave the cage in its usual place and carefully spray the cockatoo through the cage grill with an atomizer filled with water (plant sprayer that has never come in contact with insecticides). In time the cockatoo will become so comfortable with this procedure that it will make happy sounds and spread its wings in anticipation at the mere sight of the atomizer. Shower in the morning hours; this will permit the plumage to dry again by evening.

Claw Trimming: Cockatoos that are mostly kept in a cage can develop overgrown claws, despite perches with rough upper surfaces (see page 14). The bird will have difficulty grasping, and the claws must be trimmed. To do this, take the parrot in your hand, grasp its toes between two fingers, and cut the claws with a sharp nail trimmer. An untamed cockatoo must be caught (if necessary with a net and heavy leather gloves) and held firmly, while a helper trims the claws. In addition you should smooth the cut surfaces with a nail file. Avoid injuring the arteries, which extend down into the claws. In the dark cockatoo claws, the arteries are hard to see. For this reason, you should have expert claw cutting demonstrated by a veterinarian or pet dealer the first time you do it!

Beak Trimming: Overgrowth of the horn of the beak can occur if the cockatoo doesn't have enough gnawing material available (see page 15). A metabolic disturbance resulting from an unbalanced diet can also lead to malformation in the beak area, which will hinder the cockatoo's ability to eat. Only the veterinarian should undertake a beak correction.

Wing Clipping: Clipping the pinions makes sense if the bird keeps leaving its climbing branch, circles, and lands in the curtains or flowerpot, and injures itself. But consider that the shortened feathers will take a year to grow back and the cockatoo is not able to fly until then.

Cleaning the Cage and Aviary

Daily: Rinse out feed and water dishes with hot water, dry, and refill. Remove dirt around the cage with the vacuum cleaner; wipe away dust, because cockatoos shed feather dust.

Weekly: Empty droppings tray twice a week and spread with a new sand litter (see page 15).

Monthly: Thoroughly scrub the cage, droppings tray, and all the appropriate items in the cage under hot water and then dry. If you use a disinfectant, make sure it's one that is expressly for use with cage birds, possibly available through your pet

dealer or veterinarian. Follow directions exactly! For some of the disinfectants, gloves are recommended. Be sure to rinse the parrot cage thoroughly and dry out well before returning the cockatoo. Watch for strong odors; birds don't like them!

The ability to climb is noteworthy in most cockatoo species. This Goffin's cockatoo hangs upside down on the branch and "walks" along it like a gymnast.

Care of Aviary Birds

In contrast to the care measures of house birds, cockatoos that live in outdoor aviaries with a bird shelter need few maneuvers. Beak and claw trimming are not required as a rule, because the parrots usually have the opportunity to grind down claws and beak on the rough branches of different sizes. Beak growth is regulated naturally by gnawing natural wooden branches and nest boxes.

Showering: Although the cockatoos in the outdoor aviary can bathe in a rain shower or a bath that is placed at their disposal, installation of a sprinkler system is recommended for larger aviaries. During the warm summer months the system is turned on daily for a short time around midday. The plumage of the cockatoos will dry again by evening.

Small Wounds: In flight, a cockatoo often bangs against the fencing of the flight cage and so injures the sensitive skin of the nose. Also, bites on the toes acquired in fighting with rivals are not infrequent. Although sometimes such wounds bleed a great deal, it usually isn't necessary to call in the veterinarian. Rather, leave the injured bird completely at rest to give the bleeding a chance to stop. If this does not happen within a few minutes,

Wing clipping. Trim the secondaries and the inner primaries (the white portion of feathers) on both wings. Never clip just one wing! The cockatoo will be unbalanced and fall to the ground.

however, apply "Stay" (Mardel Laboratories, Inc.) immediately as birds have a small total blood volume. Excessive blood loss can lead quickly to stress, weakness, breathing difficulties, unconsciousness, and death.

Cleaning the Bird Shelter and the Flight Cage

Daily: Remove leftover food; clean feed and water dishes with hot water, dry, and refill.

Weekly: Rake out earth and sand covering and, if necessary, spread a layer of clean sand.

Monthly: The perches will be gnawed away relatively quickly by the cockatoos' strong beaks. Although this saves a cleaning, regular changing is required. Storing natural branches is advisable.

Every Six Months: Completely change the floor litter; scrub the floor of the flight cage, disinfect (see page 21), and spread with a layer of clean sand.

Yearly: Major cleaning; wash down even the flight caging and the walls of the bird shelter; if necessary apply a new layer of paint.

Important: During the cleaning and disinfection, the parrots must be removed to another place and returned to the aviary when the shelter is dry.

Table of Dangers

Source of Danger	Consequences	How to Avoid
Adhesives	Poisoning with fatal outcome caused by volatile solvents.	Remove all animals from the room when using adhesives (repairing, model making, laying floors) and ventilate very well after the work is finished.
Bathroom	Escaping through opened window. Drowning by falling into open toilet, sink, or tub. Poisoning from cleaning materials and chemicals	Keep parrots out of the bathroom; never leave the bathroom door open.
Cage grill	Strangling or getting stuck in grill with openings that are too large. Injuries to toes and head on thin, sharp-edged wire.	Choose a mesh size and a wire gauge that are appropriate for the size of the bird and examine the cage grill regularly.
Cigarettes	Smoky air is injurious. Nicotine is fatal.	It's best not to smoke in the vicinity of the bird, but at least air the surroundings regularly (avoid drafts!). Cigarettes should be kept out of the bird's reach.
Cracks (for example, between the wall and a bureau)	Getting stuck often results in death by heart failure from the bird's frantic, vain attempts to get free.	Build in chests, or pull them far enough away from walls; close all other cracks and crevices.
Doors	Caught or crushed in a carelessly closed or opened door. Escaping.	Accidents and escape can be avoided only with the greatest vigilance.
Drafts	Colds.	Avoid drafts as much as possible; in an outdoor aviary set up a windbreak.
Electric wires	Shock from gnawing or biting through wires; often fatal.	Conceal wires under trim and carpets and behind furniture, or cover with metal shields; pull plugs.
Kitchen	Steam and fumes injure the respiratory passages. Overheated kitchens and necessary ventilation lead to colds and other illnesses. Burns from hot burners and hot food in open containers.	Don't keep the bird in the kitchen, or else ventilate it regularly—be careful, however, that there are no drafts. Do not leave hot burners or pots uncovered.
Large parrots (in an aviary)	Fighting and wounds; fatal in exceptional cases.	Never leave birds of different large species together unsupervised.

Table of Dangers

Source of Danger	Consequences	How to Avoid
Other birds (rivals)	Fierce fighting. Development of stress; promotion of psychological illness (see Health and Illness, page 31).	Carefully introduce birds to other birds in aviary and observe them until a pattern of dominance, which is tolerable for all birds, has evolved.
Pets, large (dogs, cats)	Fighting and wounds; fatal in exceptional cases.	Never allow unknown animals in the vicinity of the birds or the aviary.
Plate glass	Flying against it, resulting in concussion or broken neck.	Cover plate glass (windows, balcony doors, glass walls) with curtains or accustom the parrot to what is for it invisible room boundaries: lower shades to two thirds, increase the uncovered surface a bit each day.
Poisons	Potentially lethal disturbances by tin, verdigris, nicotine, mercury, plastic-coated cookware, adhesives, cleaning materials and insecticides; harmful are pencil leads, ballpoint and felt-tip pens, alcohol, coffee, and strong spices.	Remove all poisonous items from the bird's environment, or prevent it from reaching them. Be particularly careful about lead curtain weights—parrots like to gnaw on them; remove weights, if this is possible.
Poisonous trees, bushes, houseplants	Severe disturbances, often fatal.	Don't give the bird any branches of poisonous trees or bushes to gnaw. For example, the following are poisonous: acacia, yew, laburnum, viburnum, black honeysuckle, holly, dwarf elder, and many of the needle evergreens. Keep the parrot from nibbling or eating houseplants.
Sharp objects (wires, nails, wood splinters)	Wounds, punctures, swallowing.	Don't leave anything lying around; be careful when building cages and attaching fencing for the aviary not to let any nail points protrude.
Temperature changes	Catching cold or freezing at lower temperatures, for example, if the heat goes off.	Avoid abrupt changes of temperature as much as possible; continually check the heating system; insulate the bird house.

Proper Diet

The diet of free cockatoos is quite varied, depending on their habitat. Some cockatoo species have developed specialized diets. Those that live in the grasslands of interior Australia mainly eat small seeds, including wheat field kernels found in cultivated areas.

Cockatoos that live in the tropical rain forests are not specialized feeders, for they find quite a varied diet in their natural habitat at all seasons of the year.

Such species, including the majority of those discussed in this book (see Frequently Kept Cockatoo Species, page 45), can get used to a substitute feed in captivity without any problems.

Basic Feed

The basic feed consists of various seeds, which the cockatoos receive all year round. A suitable feed mixture, which we have been using for our parrots for years, consists of 30 percent thistle seed, 30 percent sunflower kernels, 15 percent various types of millet, and 5 percent each of oats, wheat, corn, pumpkin seeds, and buckwheat (all available from pet shops). The ready-made feed mixtures offered for large parrots should not be used for maintaining cockatoos unless they are modified. The proportion of fatty sunflower seed kernels in the majority of these feed mixtures is too high for a healthy, varied large-parrot diet. Reducing the portion of sunflower seed kernels and mixing in other seeds is strongly recommended. Acorns, walnuts, hazel nuts, and Brazil nuts should be given only as treats.

Fruit, Green Feed, Sprouted Feed

Fruit, green feed, and soaked seeds (sprouted feed) contain important vitamins and minerals and are therefore essential for cockatoos.

Fruit and Vegetables: After becoming accli-mated, parrots will eat all fruits and vegetables that the store or your own garden has to offer: apples, pears, plums, peaches, pomegranates, raisins, cherries, grapes, but they also do not reject exotic fruits such as oranges, bananas, mangos, papayas, or kiwis. In addition, berry fruits of all kinds (strawberries, cranberries, blueberries, gooseberries, or red currants and mountain ash berries) as well as rose hips, are acceptable. Among the vegetables and greens, they like carrots and carrot tops, cucumbers, spinach, broccoli, celery, sweet potatoes, corn on the cob, pea pods and pieces of pumpkin and zucchini.

Note: For some cockatoos, the fresh corn kernels full of milk that grow in the fields in the fall are special treats. Any farmer is sure to be ready to part with a small quantity for a trifling amount of money.

Green Feed Plants: The palette of suitable green feeds ranges from garden vegetables (spinach, lettuce, or chard) to countless wild plants, such as shepherd's purse, chickweed, and dandelion.

During feeding the cockatoo uses its foot like a hand to hold onto larger pieces of food.

Proper Diet

Caution: Gather and feed only those weeds that you can identify and that are expressly recommended for feeding caged birds (See Useful Literature and Addresses, page 59). Don't gather wild plants along the roadside. They are polluted with automobile exhaust! Wash all fruit and vegetables thoroughly before feeding them; they may have been sprayed with insecticides.

Sprouted Feed: In winter, when there is no green feed and fruit is expensive, sprouted feed can fulfill the cockatoos' vitamin and mineral requirements. Appropriate seeds are oats, wheat, and sprouted or soaked small seeds, such as those sold for parakeets. Each type of seed is sprouted separately and then combined in one dish at feeding time.

Producing Sprouted Feed: Place a two-days' supply of seeds (see page 25) in a dish, cover them with water, and let the seed kernels soak in a warm place for 24 hours. Then shake the swollen seeds in a fine-meshed sieve while rinsing thoroughly. Now spread the seeds out on a flat screen. Put them in a warm place again. During the next 24 hours rinse the seeds thoroughly under running water several times. Depending on the degree of warmth, the seeds will have sprouted after two or three days. They should be rinsed once more and given to the cockatoos in a separate feeding dish. Give the birds only as much as they can eat within a few hours.

Caution: Sprouted feed spoils quickly, so you must remove the leftovers within a few hours, especially in summer, and clean the dish.

Animal Protein

Although cockatoos are primarily plant-eaters, their bodies also need regular supplies of animal protein in small amounts. Once a week give the cockatoo small portions of hard-boiled egg, cottage cheese, cheese, or canned dog food. Also there is nothing wrong with a discarded (raw) chop bone now and again.

Inappropriate Food

Human food, such as sausage, highly seasoned meat, chocolate, or gumdrops, is not parrot food and can be very harmful to the bird.

Rearing Feed

During the brooding period and the raising of the young, the cockatoos can be given supplementary soft food. You can easily prepare the brooding feed yourself. Use the egg feed you get from the pet shop as a basis and enrich it with grated fruit, carrots, cottage cheese, feed calcium, and vitamins. Mix them all carefully until the feed has a damp, crumbly consistency.

The rearing feed should be offered to the cockatoos in a separate feeding bowl. It's possible that the parrots will accept this strange feed only after being offered it several times. Adjustment to the food already should have taken place by the time the young hatch so that there will be no interruption in feeding while the young are being raised.

Vitamins and Minerals

Vitamin preparations are unneccessary with a balanced, varied diet. However, in winter, when there are few fruits and vegetables available, or after vacation, when the "substitute" has fed the cockatoos only with the basic necessities, it makes sense to add a multivitamin preparation (available

---

Lesser sulphur-crested cockatoo cleaning its feathers (preening). The leg plumage (above left) is just as carefully cleaned as the feathers of the wings (above right and below left). Finally the cockatoo fluffs up its plumage and shakes itself vigorously.

from the pet shop) to the drinking water.

Minerals are obtained from commercially available calcium feed, which you should sprinkle over fruit and sprouted feed weekly or mix into the brooding feed. Besides, the birds need grit and usually river sand or bird sand (see page 15), which also serves to fill the mineral requirement and to strengthen the function of the gizzard. These feed supplements are necessary for life; if they are lacking over a long period, cockatoos can even die because they cannot digest their food properly. Use the sand as cage litter (see page 15) and offer the grit in a special dish!

Drinking Water

Cockatoos need fresh tap water daily. In areas where the water quality is poor, the drinking water should be filtered or you should use uncarbonated mineral water. On warm summer days, change the drinking water twice or three times daily.

Correct Feeding

Number of Feeding Dishes: There should be at least four feeding dishes available: one will hold a wheat feed mixture, another drinking water, the third grit, and the fourth fruit, green feed, or sprouted feed in rotation. At brooding a fifth dish is needed for rearing feed.

Note: Make sure that the dishes are always clean and the cockatoos receive the same dishes in the usual order!

Feeding Time: Always feed at the the same time, either morning or afternoon. We always feed our parrots between 4 and 5 P.M., somewhat earlier in winter. They are very active at this time and can take in enough food before night falls.

Makeup of the Feed: The offered feed should consist half of dried seeds and half of green feed, fruit, and sprouted feed. Before and during the raising of young, the portion of the sprouted feed can be increased and the usual feed portion be increased by the addition of rearing feed and cooked legumes (see Cockatoo Breeding, page 35).

Quantities: The size of the daily portion varies according to the size and the mobility of the cockatoos. Cage birds who have little opportunity for exercise and smaller species (see Popular Cockatoo Species, page 45) need about 3 ounces (80 g) of seeds and about the same quantity of fruit. Larger cockatoo species and birds that live in aviaries correspondingly need more food. Basically, don't skimp on the amount of feed, but also don't overfeed regularly. The latter will produce cockatoos that are inadequately nourished because they like the taste only of the "treats."

Rose-breasted cockatoo and Goffin's cockatoo.
A rose-breasted cockatoo with erected crest (above left) and wings flexed (above right).
The Goffin's cockatoo (below) is so played out that it even lies flat on its back—unusual behavior in a bird.

Body and Wing Parts

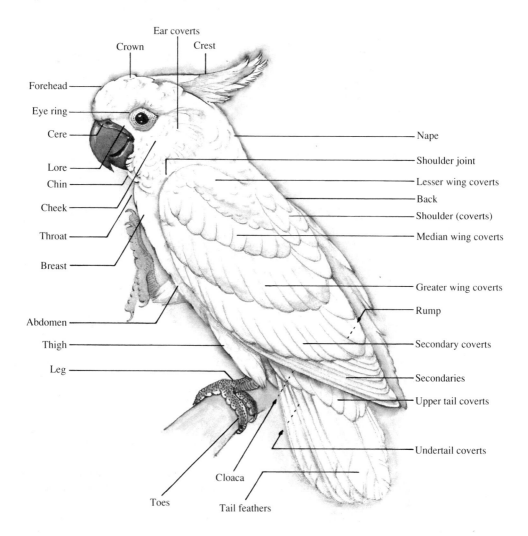

Ear coverts

Crown   Crest

Forehead ———

Eye ring ———

Cere ———

Lore ———

Chin ———

Cheek ———

Throat ———

Breast ———

Abdomen ———

Thigh ———

Leg ———

Nape

Shoulder joint

Lesser wing coverts

Back

Shoulder (coverts)

Median wing coverts

Greater wing coverts

Rump

Secondary coverts

Secondaries

Upper tail coverts

Undertail coverts

Cloaca

Toes

Tail feathers

Names of body parts of the cockatoo can be useful to know, especially if you need to visit the veterinarian.

Health and Illness

Common Signs of Illness

Properly maintained and cared for cockatoos seldom become ill. But even an experienced parrot-keeper can make a maintenance mistake once in a while, or the cockatoo's natural resistance may be weakened for some unknown reason so that it succumbs to illness. There are no specific signs of illness for most parrot ailments, but nevertheless it is apparent when a cockatoo feels sick (see Choosing a Healthy Cockatoo, page 8).

First Aid Measures

Only the experienced parrot-keeper is in a position to judge whether a parrot's illness is of a serious or mild nature. Novice parrot-keepers should always consult an avian veterinarian promptly.

A sick cockatoo must be separated immediately from the other parrots and removed to an individual cage (quarantine cages offered by pet dealers are excellent).

An effective first-aid measure for mild illnesses is therapy with infrared light, which also is recommended and used by veterinarians.

Place the infrared lamp at a distance of about 23 inches (60 cm) from the cage, directed to penetrate half the cage only so the bird can move to a cooler temperature zone if the lamp gets too warm.

The Visit to the Avian Veterinarian

If the condition of the cockatoo does not improve within a day, a trip to the veterinarian is unavoidable. Find out at the time you get your cockatoo which veterinarians have the required experience in treating parrots.

Transporting the bird must be done with as much protection for the bird as possible. This can generally be best accomplished by using a transport box (padded if this proves to be necessary).

The doctor's questions about maintenance conditions, the bird's behavior, and the signs of illness should be answered precisely. This will make the diagnosis substantially easier.

A fecal sample from the bird (if possible fresh and unmixed with sand) is sometimes very helpful for a precise diagnosis. It probably should be examined at the outset.

Treatment usually will be started by the doctor at once; he or she prescribes medications and advises care measures for the sick bird.

Successful healing is guaranteed only if you follow the veterinarian's instructions exactly. For instance, stopping the treatment too early not uncommonly leads to severe relapses.

Common Illnesses

Infestation with Ectoparasites (External Parasites)

Parrots can be attacked by mites, feather mites, or lice. The parasites live on the body surfaces and in the plumage of the infested birds. In well-kept parrots the infestation is very seldom of any great extent.

Symptoms: The infested bird is restless, preens markedly often and for prolonged periods, and scratches itself frequently with its toes and beak, because it is irritated constantly by itching. Gradually bare spots appear on the head, abdomen, and under the wings.

Possible Causes: Repeated neglect of cleaning procedures; other causes are possible (ask the veterinarian).

Treatment: Dust the bird with a suitable flea and tick powder containing pyrethrin or cabaryl (ask advice of the pet dealer or veterinarian) and treat the entire living area.

Caution: To avoid severe poisoning, strictly observe the following precautions:

Health and Illness

- Use only an insecticide that the manufacturer has stated expressly to be suitable for cage birds.
- When dusting, protect the bird's eyes, nose, and beak carefully with your hand.
- Never treat a bird with a spray.
- When the cages are being dusted, always remove all birds.

Prevention: Regular, thorough cleaning of the cage area, making sure that all wooden parts are scrubbed down with hot water and a disinfectant.

Infestation with Endoparasites (Internal Parasites)

Parrots are mainly attacked by tapeworms (Cestoda), roundworms (Ascaridia), and threadworms (Capillaria).

Symptoms: There are no typical symptoms; the ailing bird sits around, often with ruffled feathers, slowly wastes away, and deposits slimy feces. Sudden death can occur as a result of intestinal obstruction by hundreds of worms (usually roundworms).

Possible Causes: Dirty maintenance conditions promote the illness.

Immediate Measures: Fecal examination at the appearance of the first sign of illness (proper treatment can lessen the extent and the consequences of the worm infestation).

Treatment: By the veterinarian, who is the only one who can prescribe appropriate medication (Yomesan); follow the dosage instructions exactly. An overdose can be dangerous for the parrot.

Prevention: Regularly clean the bird cages and houses thoroughly. The droppings of parrots that live in an outdoor cage should be examined several times a year for worms.

Intestinal Inflammation

One of the most frequent parrot ailments.

Symptoms: General signs of illness (see page 31), diarrhea, increased water intake (as a result of high fluid loss), diminished food intake, so that this illness can sometimes mean a serious threat to the life of the parrot.

Note: Psychological factors can lead to diarrhea-like bowel movements, which should not be considered the result of an intestinal inflammation. For example, the sight of a predatory bird flying in the air or of a cat lurking on the roof of the aviary, anxiety at being caught by the keeper, or an encounter with a rival bird can lead to sudden, watery diarrhea.

Possible Causes: Spoiled feed, change of diet, intake of poisonous material (for example lead, lead weights in curtains, plastic ties as for bread bags, varnish, cleaning materials), colds, bacterial infections i.e., E. Coli and Salmonella), fungi, viruses, parasites, tumors, diseases of other organs, and practically any type of medication.

Immediate Measures: If you suspect poisoning (especially by lead!), get to the doctor immediately. Otherwise offer camomile tea, some Kaopectate or Pepto Bismol, and easily digested food, and infrared treatment (see page 31). If the bird seems very weak or the first-aid measures don't lead to improvement within a few hours, take a fecal sample and go to the veterinarian as quickly as possible.

Treatment: The veterinarian must order a course of medication. Follow instructions exactly!

Prevention: Avoid causes or constantly check maintenance.

Coccidiosis

Coccidia are one-celled intestinal parasites (protozoa) that live in the mucous membranes of the intestinal tract of the parrot.

Symptoms: Coccidia can produce severe inflammation of the mucous membrane; this produces intestinal bleeding, accompanied by diarrhea and weight loss.

Possible Causes: Unclean housing conditions and poor physical condition of the bird promote the illness.

Treatment: Only by the veterinarian.

Prevention: Regular, thorough cleaning and disinfection of the cage (according to directions), fecal examination—important because if treatment is begun early, the bird can be free of coccidia in a shorter time.

Respiratory Ailments

Dysfunctions of the respiratory organs can result from very different causes. A diagnosis is exceedingly important but is sometimes impossible in a living bird.

Symptoms: General signs of illness (see page 31), repeated sneezing, damp or stuffed-up nostrils, discharge from the nose, labored breathing (the bird sits with legs spread, breathes with open beak, and the tail moves conspicuously up and down with every breath), noisy breathing; occasionally conjunctivitis of the eyelid also occurs.

Possible Causes: Attack on the respiratory passages by bacteria, virus, or fungus; cold from drafts or wrong or suddenly changed maintenance temperature; other causes are also possible.

Immediate Measures: Infrared treatment (see page 31). If there is no improvement after 12 hours, the parrot needs a veterinarian's help. With serious breathing difficulty or noisy breathing, get to the avian veterinarian at once!

Treatment: Only by the doctor. Starting treatment promptly can increase the chance of cure. But not every case can be successfully treated.

Feather Eating, Feather Plucking

An uncommon manifestation, which probably belongs to the psychological illnesses. It primarily is encountered in the singly kept parrot, but can also occur with pairs and in optimal maintenance conditions.

Symptoms: Ranges from constant pulling out and chewing of single contour feathers, especially in the shoulder, inner wing, or breast area, to the complete stripping of the body (with the exception of the unreachable head feathers). Cases of self-mutilation, even to the extent that the skin or the underlying musculature are gnawed, have also been reported.

Possible Causes: Not known for certain; until more is determined, we assume that the coinciding of several of the following factors triggers, or at least promotes, feather eating or feather plucking:

• Insufficient exercise; too small cage.
• Boredom in "sterile" accommodations.
• Prolonged stress under overcrowded conditions in a cage or aviary, and lack of sleep.
• Lack of or loss of a favorite person.
• Lack of a mate at the beginning of sexual maturity.
• Skin ailment that causes itching, or heavy molt.
• Inadequate diet, wrong temperature in the environment, insufficient humidity.
• Lack of opportunity for bathing or lack of regular showering.

Feather pluckers. Cockatoos that pull out their feathers to the point of almost complete baldness usually have psychological ailments.

Treatment: Avoid faulty care and maintenance! Frequently remove the feathers that fall to the bottom of the cage. In some cases it is advisable to transfer the affected parrot from a cage to a larger aviary complete with extensive opportunities for exercise in the form of gnawing branches, chains, wooden toys, rope ends, or climbing apparatus; if necessary put the bird with a companion bird. Pay attention to your single bird more often and more intensively! Allow the bird 8 to 12 hours of sleep in a darkened room. Consult an avian veterinarian who may prescribe steroids, tranquilizers, and hormones.

Scratching with a foot is a part of preening.

Prevention: Optimal living conditions. In cases of single birds, sufficient attention; better still the provision of a mate.

Note: Since about 1980, a plumage disease (cockatoo syndrome or psittacine beak and feather syndrome) has been reported, which at this time has been certainly confirmed in the so-called white cockatoo, but also may occur in cockatiels and other species. In its beginning stages this illness is similar to feather plucking. The feathers that normally regrow during molting appear to be incompletely formed, the plumage becomes increasingly full of holes, until finally the growth of feathers comes to a halt. The cockatoo is unable to fly. In addition a softening of the beak can be observed in some cases.

It has been suggested that the cause is a virus infection that is promoted by stress; other factors have not been ruled out. However, definite information about the cause of the illness at this time is lacking, as is knowledge of possible treatments. Affected cockatoos frequently die within several months.

Parrot Fever (Psittacosis)

Parrot fever or psittacosis is by no means one of the common illnesses of parrots. Nevertheless, it should be discussed briefly because the name is very familiar to lay-people and it can produce serious and to some degree life-threatening symptoms in parrots and humans. Psittacosis is an infectious illness, which is not limited only to parrots. The microorganism that causes this disease has been identified in more than a hundred other bird species (the term ornithosis is used in these cases).

Symptoms: No characteristic symptoms. Sleepiness, weight loss, diarrhea, inflammation of eye membranes, and diminished food intake can be concomitant signs of the illness.

Treatment: According to public-health laws, the disease must be reported and must be treated. Affected parrots are placed in isolation according to the instructions of the public health officer and treated with an appropriate antibiotic.

Note: For humans, a psittacosis infection can become a life-threatening illness. Besides moderate symptoms, similar to those of a cold or flu, severe illness with high fever and infection of the respiratory organs also has been observed. The disease is curable if it is recognized and treated in time.

Prevention: Scarcely possible; it is important that the parrot be acquired disease-free (you will find full information about psittacosis in textbooks and journals, see page 59). Be careful about buying parrots kept in crowded cages and under unhygienic conditions.

Cockatoo Breeding

Greater and lesser sulphur-crested and rose-breasted cockatoos breed in human captivity the best of all the large parrot species—provided they have the right living conditions. To be successful with breeding, you must provide some basic requirements (especially in living arrangements and diet).

Species Protection

Cockatoos are among the species of animals that are endangered or threatened with extinction. The cause of this is the ongoing destruction of their habitat. Expanses of forest are being recklessley destroyed in order to gain usable land area, and with them the breeding and sleeping trees of many cockatoo species are also falling victim to the power saw.

However, the animal trade also is not entirely without blame for the shrinkage of the cockatoo population in nature. Because the number of cockatoos bred in captivity is very small, wild cockatoos are caught and sold by the thousands to bird fanciers all over the world.

According to the Washington Endangered Species Convention, trade in cockatoos in the United States and Europe has become more difficult (see Formalities of Purchase, page 12). But this alone does not guarantee the preservation of many cockatoo species. Successful conservation can be achieved only with the combination of species protection by law and purposeful cockatoo breeding by zoos and fanciers.

Prerequisites for Successful Breeding

Housing: Housing a cockatoo pair in a bird room (see page 14) or in an outdoor aviary (see page 16) offers the best conditions for successful breeding. If several parrots are kept together it's better to put the pair in a separate aviary section that is somewhat removed from family comings and goings or traffic noise. If you have a system of several aviaries together, you should make sure that the breeding pair isn't disturbed by neighbor birds during its courtship preparations (erect screens if necessary).

During mating the female "lies" flat on the perch with wings folded indicating her receptiveness to copulation.

Additions to the Diet During Breeding: If you feed your cockatoos a balanced, varied diet (see Proper Diet, page 25), nutrient supplements before and during breeding are unnecessary as a rule. Only when the diet is unbalanced should breeding birds be offered rearing feed (see page 26). Nevertheless, it's a good idea to maintain a certain seasonal rhythm in the composition of the feed. For birds you plan to use for breeding:

• During the winter months use corn as the basic feed, and add fruit and greenstuff.
• Then in spring, use less corn in the basic feed and add boiled legumes, sprouted seeds, and various

Cockatoo Breeding

kinds of fruit.

Nest Boxes: The nest box should have a square base (see drawing, page 40) and can be obtained in the recommended size (see size table, page 40) from the pet store or can be made at home if you are handy with tools. Reinforce the edges of the entry hole with strips of tin, to prevent the cockatoos from expanding the entry hole with their beaks. Underneath the entrance hole (inside the box) fasten strong, wide-meshed rectangular wire fencing to serve as a climbing aid.

Brooding Hole: The brooding hole consists of a hollow tree trunk (see drawing, page 40), which you can order from the pet store.

Litter for the Nest Box: Equip nest boxes or hollow trees with a layer of wood humus about 4 inches (10 cm) thick, which should be slightly dampened shortly before the time of nesting. This way the eggs will settle properly under the weight of the female.

Mounting Nest Boxes: Nesting places are attached high under the roof of the aviary (in a garden aviary, in the roofed-over part) or in the bird shelter under the roof. If possible, place them so that you can easily examine the brooding hole or nest box without startling the birds.

Note: Cockatoos nest only at the time of brooding. After brooding, the hollow trees and nest boxes must be thoroughly cleaned, disinfected, repaired if necessary, and stored dry until the next reproduction period.

Pairing

Sex determination is relatively simple for the species described here (see Determining Sex, page 11). However, it is not so easy to establish a harmonious pair. All birds intended for breeding should belong to the same species or subspecies. Grown birds can become used to each other with difficulty (see Getting Used to Each Other, page 20). On the other hand, if several young birds of different sexes live together in one aviary, a harmonious cockatoo pair will develop very quickly.

Sometimes spontaneous pairing also will occur in adult birds as it does with young birds. It also can happen, however, that two cockatoos will not adjust to each other, even after several attempts. In this case the bird must be exchanged as soon as possible.

Brooding Period

With cockatoos that are kept in an indoor aviary or in a bird room, the brooding period can occur at any season. If the parrots live in an outdoor aviary and winter over in the bird shelter, the brooding birds eventually establish a seasonal rhythm. Brooding season begins about the end of April (egg laying the beginning of May, hatching of young at the beginning of June, and young leaving the nest from the middle of July to the beginning of August, with stragglers somewhat later). Molting occurs in September and October. After that the cockatoos go into a winter rest period until the next spring.

Courtship and Mating

In many cockatoo species the courtship behavior is very impressive.

Display Behavior: With spread feathers and wings, fanned tail, and erect crest feathers, the male woos his female (see drawing, page 19). This so-called display behavior serves on one hand to scare off rival suitors, on the other to court the female (see

Bare-eyed cockatoos
A well-adjusted pair in front of their nest hole.

Cockatoo Breeding

Social Behavior, page 44).

Mutual Preening: Another courtship behavior often seen is mutual preening (see drawing, page 5), the mutual "scratching" of two birds. This behavior has a social function in that it serves to strengthen pair bonding. But also both birds can enjoy preening on places like the head or rump area that a single bird can reach only with difficulty by itself.

Copulation: Courtship usually leads to mating. The male mounts the female so that their cloacas (into which both the spermatic duct and the oviduct empty) are joined and so copulation is accomplished. Shortly before egg laying, the readiness to mate and the frequency of copulation increases.

Egg Laying and Brooding

The end of the courtship period is followed by egg laying. At intervals of two to three days—in the afternoon or early morning—the cockatoo female lays two to three uniformly white, round-oval eggs. In the species described here, the female and male take turns brooding, although the greater part of it falls to the female. Both parents can get food independently of each other from time to time. For this reason cockatoos lack the partner-feeding behavior noted in other parrots, a social pattern in which the male provides the female and the young with food during the brooding and raising periods.

The length of the brooding period, depending on the species (see Frequently Kept Cockatoo Species, page 45), is somewhere between 25 and 30 days.

Popular cockatoo species.
Leadbeater's cockatoo, bred in captivity (above left); umbrella-crested cockatoo pair (above right); citron-crested cockatoo, subspecies of the lesser sulphur-crested cockatoo (below left); rose-breasted cockatoo (below right).

Development of the Young

The young cockatoos hatch at the same intervals at which the eggs were laid. At birth they are—like all altricial birds—naked, blind, and completely helpless. Their bodily development takes a fairly long time; they open their eyes only after several weeks, and a thick coat of down develops to protect them from the cold. Between 60 and 100 days—depending on the species—the young cockatoos get their complete plumage and can leave the nest. Before they are completely independent, however, they pass a further two to three weeks in which they are cared for and fed by their parents.

Note: Cockatoos as a rule raise only one young bird out of a two- or three-egg clutch. The remaining one or two eggs are a reserve, so to speak, in case something goes wrong with the oldest nestling in the first few days. But if the firstborn bird develops normally, the feeding and care of the younger animals is sometimes neglected so that they often pine away or die prematurely. In this case, the breeder can try to raise the young birds by hand.

Hand-raising

It happens that cockatoos leave their eggs because of frequent disturbance or that they can't give enough care to all the young birds. In noticing this soon enough, the breeder can take the eggs from the nest and continue developing them in an incubator. Young birds hatched in an incubator, or nestlings that have been neglected by their parents, may be raised by hand.

A drawback to hand-raising is of course that the young birds are completely imprinted on humans and sometimes cannot be used later for breeding.

Housing: Keep the parrot chicks at a temperature of about 97°F (36°C). An infrared lamp is very good for this. Choose a container for keeping the nestling that isn't too large (a hospital cage or a wooden box with a glass front). The quarters should be controlled thermostatically. The temperature should be reduced gradually as the bird(s) mature(s).

Suitable brooding holes. Left: hollowed out tree trunk (available in pet stores); the removable peephole door on the side is closed with a metal rod. Right: homemade nest box; roof and peephole door can be lifted up.

Food and Feeding: At the beginning, the young birds get a feed gruel every two hours between 6 A.M. and 12 P.M. Powdered baby formula mixed with water is very good. At two- to three-day intervals, add vitamins and minerals to the gruel. The food must be mixed fresh daily and should have a temperature of 104° to 105.8°F (40–41°C) at feeding; in the beginning it can be administered with a large-

volume plastic eyedropper, and later with a teaspoon (the sides of which have been bent inwards). With increasing age, the young birds are fed only every three to four hours. The feed gruel may then be enriched with small pieces of cut-up egg yolk, fruit, and greenstuff. The food can be offered to the growing cockatoos at room temperature or even lukewarm.

It is difficult to manage the crossover from feed gruel to grain feed. Get the young cockatoos used to it step by step. At first give them the familiar gruel in the feeding dish, then later soft fruit and greenery, and finally seeds, first ground up or hulled, then whole. Teaching the young cockatoos how to remove the hulls of the seeds properly is best accomplished by its watching older neighboring birds. Be careful to see that the young birds are never subject to sudden temperature changes or drafts. Only when they are fully feathered should cockatoo young be kept at room temperature without any additional heat source.

What to Watch Out for During Brooding.

Brooding is an exceptional situation for the cockatoos as well as for the breeder; therefore:

Nest Box Measurements

Species	Nest Box Height (inches [cm])	Internal Diameter of Natural Trunk (inches [cm])	Length of Side of Square Wooden Box (inches [cm])	Diameter of Entry Hole (inches [cm])
Goffin's Philippine cockatoo	23–31 (60–80)	10–12 (25–30)	10 (25)	4 (10)
Lesser sulphur-crested, bare-eyed, rose-breasted cockatoo	31–39 (80–100)	12–14 (30–35)	12 (30)	4–5 (10–12)
Moluccan, umbrella-crested, greater sulphur-crested cockatoo	47–59 (120–150)	14–18 (34–45)	14 (35)	5–6 (12–15)

Cockatoo Breeding

• If possible don't enter the aviary during the brooding period, for some cockatoos become very aggressive and will attack.

• Avoid disturbances, such as building alterations or large cleaning operations, and keep visitors from the brooding birds.

• Before and during the raising of the young, provide a variety of feed in sufficient quantities.

• In especially dry summer months the nest boxes must be sprayed with water on the outside every so often.

• Make sure that the brooding birds always have an opportunity to bathe.

Developmental stages of a young greater sulphur-crested cockatoo—day 25 through day 40.

At 25 days—their eyes are open and the quills have begun to break through the skin

At about five weeks—the quills can be seen on the head, and the beak darkens in color.

At 40 days—their yellow crest feathers are visible and a portion of the wing and back plumage has appeared.

Understanding Cockatoos

How Cockatoos Live Together in Nature

Quite a bit is known about the way of life and the behavior of cockatoos in their natural habitat—in contrast to most of the other parrot species.

Group Size: The cockatoo species that are described in this book live together in flocks except during the brooding period. Such flocks consist of single animals, pairs, and families that gather at common eating, drinking, and sleeping places. While searching for food, cockatoos—particularly those of the plains and desert habitats—congregate in large groups. Often one will encounter groups of several thousand birds at favorite spots. In contrast, groups of those species that are found in the tropical rain forests outside the Australian continent are much smaller, containing only eight to ten birds.

The Communal Life: Gathering into groups functions primarily to ensure that the cockatoos will find food. Meeting social needs cannot be assumed to be an important function because the birds in the group don't usually enter into any closer social bonds—except for the choice of mate. Rather, the communal life can be characterized as a kind of open association in which the individual animals don't necessarily know each other and in which there is no firmly defined order of dominance. The advantage of a federation is that feeding places can be better scouted and can be secured against rival feeders. Of course there are also frequent quarrels within the cockatoo association about the best feeding places, sleeping places, and nest holes.

Brooding Season: Among cockatoos the urge to brood is dependent on the environmental conditions. This means that the birds will be impelled to breed when the plant growth has reached its height and also when the weather conditions are best. Pairs that are ready to breed separate from the group and go searching for nest holes. Rotted-out tree trunks or abandoned woodpecker holes serve as brooding holes. Usually the holes are enlarged with the cockatoo's strong beak. The shavings that fall into the hole as a result of this process are used by the cockatoos as a bed for their eggs. As a rule they don't bring in additional nest material. The cockatoos of the tropical rain forests of the Indonesian islands set about breeding after the rainy season and try to occupy the same nest holes every year. Cockatoo species that inhabit the arid areas of the Australian interior lead a nomadic or partially nomadic life. Presumably they breed yearly—according to the food supply—in various districts. Egg laying, clutch size, and brooding time vary from species to species. After the young hatch, the parent cockatoos are busy raising them for many weeks. Afterwards the parents and their young join as a family group with other cockatoos in a close flock, which remains in existence until the next breeding season.

Important Behavior Patterns of Cockatoos

To help you better understand your cockatoos and correctly interpret their behavior, we offer the following descriptions of the most frequent behavior patterns and movements.

Eating and Drinking

The cockatoo removes the hulls from seeds in its beak with its tongue. It reduces fruit and green feed with its beak. Like most large parrots, the cockatoo uses its foot like a hand, to hold morsels of food and lift food to its beak. To drink, the bird scoops up water with its lower beak and tips its head back to swallow.

Resting and Sleeping

Healthy birds rest and sleep on one leg; the other leg is drawn up into the feathers. The body plumage is fluffed slightly, the head is usually turned back and tucked into the back feathers to the base of the beak. The eyes may be either closed completely or partially.

Understanding Cockatoos

Types of Movement

Cockatoos that live in captivity are in nearly constant motion all day long. In the cage they climb and do gymnastics tirelessly; in outdoor aviaries you find them almost constantly climbing, scratching, gnawing, or flying. Besides their natural motions, with training cockatoos also are able to mimic playful movements. There are cockatoos that can carry things, push little toy cars, eat from a spoon, and much more.

Running: Cockatoos, especially those of the dry plains and grasslands of interior Australia, are "good on their feet," for they find their food predominantly on the ground. Birds of these species

Threatening behavior. Similar to courtship behavior, the cockatoo "displays" with erected crest feathers, spread wings, and fanned tail—signalling readiness for attack to the enemy or rival.

also can be observed frequently running in the aviary or cage. The cockatoo's body is held erect as it runs with long, stiff-gaited steps.

Scratching: Some cockatoo species love to scratch. This behavior pattern has developed because they find their food mainly on the ground. The

most noticeable adaptation to this form of food seeking is seen in the slender-billed cockatoo, which has an elongated upper beak suitable for digging.

Climbing: Most cockatoo species possess excellent climbing ability. Therefore you should offer your cockatoo plenty of things to climb in the cage and in the aviary.

Flying: In their natural habitat, many cockatoo species often cover long distances in their search for feeding places. They are excellent fliers. In captivity, a cockatoo especially enjoys the chance to fly in the apartment and also in the outdoor aviary or bird room. In free flight it becomes clear what nimble fliers these parrots are. You can easily imagine the degree of psychological torture for the cockatoo that is kept for any length of time in a cage that is much too small.

Comfort Behavior

Comfort behavior includes patterns concerned with the body care of the cockatoo.

Preening: A cockatoo preens its plumage several times daily by drawing individual feathers through its beak. The bird usually begins with the smaller feathers, then polishes the primaries and secondaries and the tail feathers. Finally, by means of rubbing movements with the head and beak, the bird distributes the feather dust over its plumage.

Head Scratching: Also as part of plumage care, the bird lifts its foot to its head and scratches while turning and twisting its head. Some cockatoos occasionally use little branches to help scratch. An unusual behavior is the slow, hesitant, almost slow-motion head scratching, that rather looks like someone swimming the crawl. This behavior is primarily seen in single birds—perhaps satisfying its need for mutual preening (see page 39) with a partner bird in this way.

Beak Care: The cockatoo removes dirt and food particles from its beak by rubbing it on a hard surface, such as the perch.

Showering: All cockatoos love to take shower

Understanding Cockatoos

baths when they get used to the procedure. They spread their wings slightly and fan their tails. During the shower they twist and turn their whole body and flap their wings so that the feathers get damp all over.

Stretching: Stretching movements, often accompanied by yawns, frequently are observable after rest periods. The wing and leg on the same side of the body will be stretched to the rear/down, while at the same time the corresponding side of the tail will be spread. Sometimes you will also see the bird lifting both wings over its back and spreading them. Yawning stretches the beak parts, though this serves primarily to supply the body with oxygen.

Social Behavior

Even before the onset of sexual maturity the cockatoo develops social contacts, which in time lead to pair bonding.

Courtship Behavior

The behavior patterns of courtship serve to promote the formation of a cockatoo pair and the strengthening of this bond. The courtship behavior of young and inexperienced cockatoos is especially striking.

Display Behavior: Display behavior (see Courtship and Mating, page 36) is a kind of forerunner of true courtship. The male shows off his body to the chosen female. With spread tail, opened wings, ruffled feathers, and sometimes erected crest, whose colors also serve as a warning signal to rivals, the male makes himself noticeable. The display is accompanied by choppy, "angular" movements, and a backward lifting and sinking of the body on the perch. This striking behavior—besides wooing the female—is supposed to frighten off rival males and keep them away from the female. Display therefore serves partly as threatening behavior. At first the female repulses the male's attempts to approach and avoids mating. In time however she permits the male in her vicinity.

Mutual Preening: During the courtship period the mutual scratching that is termed mutual preening has a calming, aggression-checking function. It allows the birds to get used to increasingly intensive contact, until finally copulation occurs.

Copulation: During copulation the male mounts the female and they mate through the joining of the anal opening. Between adult mates that already have several successful broods, the preliminary courtship may be shortened greatly, and in some instances spontaneous copulation may occur. Often the female invites her partner to mate.

Threatening Behavior: Threatening behavior is very similar to display behavior. In general, threat and aggression toward presumed enemies or rivals increases with growing breeding urge. Snapping the beak and lateral presentation (forebody lowered, tail lifted, and tail feathers spread) also express an aggressive mood.

Popular Cockatoo Species

Interesting Facts about Cockatoos

Parrots constitute some 320–330 of the approximately 8,600 bird species on the earth. In the order of parrots there are 18 cockatoo species, including the cockatiels.

Like the majority of parrots, cockatoos have a powerful, mobile curved beak and a distinctive toe formation (two toes point forward, two rearward). Their mostly white or dark plumage and their long, movable forehead and crown feathers (pointed, broad, and rounded crests) distinguish them visually from the other parrots.

Distribution: Cockatoos are distributed over wide areas of Australia and Indonesia. The Philippine cockatoo has the northernmost distribution area. It inhabits the Philippine island of Luzon (19° north latitude). The funereal cockatoo and the greater sulphur-crested cockatoo have the southernmost ranges. Both species, along with others, are found on Tasmania. Cockatoos inhabit three environments: tropical rain forests with high temperatures and heavy rainfall; grassy plains as transition zones between rain forests and desert (humid and dry savannahs); and wastes with prairie-like vegetation and scant, irregular rainfall.

Cockatoo Species: The species described in this book are indicated with an asterisk.

Family: *Cacatuidae*—cockatoos
Subfamily: *Cacatuinae*—true cockatoos

Genus: *Probosciger*
Species: Palm cockatoo (*P. aterrimus*, five subspecies)

Genus: *Calyptorhynchus*
Species: Red-tailed black or Banksian cockatoo (*C. magnificus*, four subspecies)
Glossy black cockatoo (*C. lathami*)
Funereal or yellow-tailed black cockatoo (*C. funereus*, three subspecies)
White-tailed black or Baudin's black cockatoo (*C. baudinii*, four subspecies)

Genus: *Callocephalon*
Species: Gang-gang or red-crowned or helmeted cockatoo (*C. fimbriatum*)

Genus: *Eolophus*
Species: Rose-breasted or roseate cockatoo, galah* (*E. roseicapillus,* three subspecies)

Genus: *Cacatua*
Species: Philippine or red-vented cockatoo* (*C. haematuropygia*)
Goffin's cockatoo* (*C. goffini*)
Bare-eyed cockatoo or little corella* (*C. sanguinea*, two subspecies)
Slender-billed cockatoo (*C. tenuirostris*, two subspecies)
Ducorp's cockatoo (*C. ducorps*)
Blue-eyed cockatoo, (*C. ophthalmica*)
Greater sulphur-crested cockatoo*(*C. galerita*, four subspecies)
Lesser sulphur-crested cockatoo*(*C. sulphurea*, six subspecies)
Umbrella-crested, white-crested or greater white-crested cockatoo* (*C. alba*)
Moluccan cockatoo* (*C. moluccensis*)
Leadbeater's cockatoo (*C. leadbeateri*, four subspecies)

Frequently Kept Cockatoo Species

Altogether, there are only eight cockatoo species that are usually imported and available commercially. A detailed description of each of these species follows.

Rose-breasted or Roseate Cockatoo, or Galah

Eolophus roseicapillus (3 subspecies)
[Photographs pages: 28, 38, 46, back cover]

Description: Total length 13½ inches (35 cm).

Popular Cockatoo Species

Male: upper side gray, underside rose-red; forehead, crown, neck, and crest feathers pale pink, almost white; undertail coverts gray; tail underside gray-black; beak yellowish gray; legs gray; iris dark brown to black. Female: similar to male but iris red to red-brown.

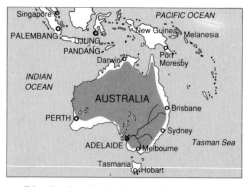

Distribution: Entire interior of Australian continent.

Habitat: Primarily dry areas, but also other forms of climate and vegetation; frequently in the vicinity of artificially-created water areas, in parks and gardens.

Maintenance: Among the most coveted, hunted, and expensive parrots. Because of the high purchase price they seldom are kept as house pets. Usually they are kept by breeders, who house these skillful flyers in roomy aviaries; as aviary birds they are relatively undemanding and exceptionally climate-resistant. Rose-breasted cockatoos do not have as great a need to gnaw or as loud a voice as most other cockatoo species.

Breeding: Often successful. In courtship the male struts up to the female, bows his head forward, and raises his crest. A brief chattering of the beak accompanies wooing. Before egg laying the females line the nest box with small branches and leaves. The clutch consists of 3 to 4 eggs, which are brooded by both parents taking turns for 25 days. After about 7 weeks the young leave the nest box. Rose-breasted cockatoos are crossed with um-

brella-crested, slender-billed, greater sulphur-crested, and Leadbeater's cockatoos.

Philippine or Red-vented Cockatoo
Cacatua haematuropygia
Description: Total length 12 inches (31 cm).

Male: basic plumage color white; ear patch pale yellow; small broad crest with yellowish color at base of feathers; underwing coverts and underside of tail yellowish; rump plumage red with white margins; unfeathered eye ring white; beak gray-white; legs gray; iris black-brown. Female: similar to male, but iris red-brown to red.

Distribution: Philippine Islands including Palawan and the Sulu Islands.

Habitat: Primarily forests with primitive vegetation; only occasionally seeks open areas and wheat fields along the edges of forests for feeding.

Maintenance: Keeping the Philippine cockatoo is not apt to be problem-free. Young birds have a tendency to disturbances of plumage develop-

Cockatoos in their Australian habitat.
Red-tailed black cockatoos (above); a flock of rose-breasted cockatoos (below).

46

ment during the first major molt (see Common Illnesses, page 31), which frequently results in death. It is necessary to be especially careful when choosing a bird to buy (see Choosing a Healthy Cockatoo, page 8). The voice of the Philippine cockatoo is quite tolerable and is usually heard in the morning and evening. Roomy aviaries with heated shelters are recommended for these extraordinary flyers. They have a tendency toward feather plucking in close quarters (or when kept singly).

Breeding: Successful only occasionally; the first successful breeding in the world was done by W. Eichelberger in 1974 in Switzerland. Philippine cockatoos are choosy when looking for a mate. During the brooding period the males become very aggressive, even toward their females, and can sometimes inflict serious wounds. The clutch consists of 2 to 3 eggs. The brooding period lasts about 30 days. After some 60 days the young leave the nest box. Crossing a Philippine and a Leadbeater's cockatoo has been described.

Goffin's Cockatoo

Cacatua goffini
[Photographs: inside front cover, pages 10, 28, back cover]

Description: Total length 12½ inches (32 cm). Male: basic plumage color white; bridle pink; small rounded crest; undersides of wing and tail yellowish; unfeathered eye ring gray-white; beak whitish yellow; legs light gray; iris black. Female: similar to male except iris brown-red.

Distribution: Exclusively on Tanimbar Island off New Guinea.

Australian rose-breasted cockatoos drinking in flight.
The cockatoo flies down and sinks its head (above); it dips its beak into the water to drink and starts up again immediately (below). A photo series by animal filmmakers Arendt and Schweiger.

Habitat: Primarily forest.

Maintenance: One of the smallest cockatoos, it appears not to be very popular among parrot fanciers; very little has been reported about it over the last ten years. Goffin's cockatoos offer no problems in maintenance and are undemanding. They can be wintered over in a dry, draft-free, slightly heated bird house. Nevertheless, Goffin's cockatoos have a strong need to gnaw and a relatively loud voice. In confined living conditions, even when kept in pairs, they have a tendency toward feather plucking. A single bird can become very tame and learns to imitate different clever tricks.

Breeding: Rarely successful; the first successful German attempt was made in 1978 by Th. Weise

PACIFIC OCEAN	New Guinea	Port Moresby
Coral Sea Cairns	AUSTRALIA	Darwin
Arafura Sea Moluccas	Sunda Islands	INDONESIA
UJUNG PANDANG	Celebes (Sulawesi)	Manado
Celebes Sea		

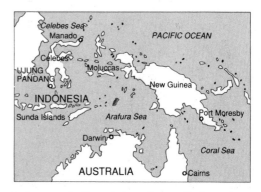

in Dortmund. These little cockatoos display rather inconspicuous courtship behavior, which is accompanied (in both sexes) by chattering of the beak. The clutch consists of 2 to 3 eggs. The brooding period runs 26 to 28 days. It is not known exactly when the young leave the nest box. Accounts on record range from 60 to 85 days.

Popular Cockatoo Species

Bare-eyed Cockatoo or Little Corella

Cacatua sanguinea (2 subspecies)
[Photograph: page 37]

Description: Total length 15½ inches (40 cm). Male and female: basic plumage color white with reddish tinges on forehead, crown, neck, and throat areas; small rounded crest; blue-gray unfeathered eye ring; beak horn-colored to white; legs gray; iris in both sexes dark brown to black. Female is usually smaller than the male.

Distribution: The nominate form in eastern, north-western, and northern Australia, the subspecies *Cacatua sanguinea normantoni* in parts of southern New Guinea.

Habitat: Primarily dry inland areas; open coun-

try along river courses is favored, unbroken forests largely avoided. Like the rose-breasted cockatoo the bare-eyed cockatoo has followed humankind into the gardens and parks and sometimes inflicts great damage on the grain-growing areas.

Maintenance: Because Australia has banned the export of all plant and animal species since 1960, trade is almost exclusively in animals from the subspecies *Cacatua sanguinea normantoni*, which stems from New Guinea. Young birds quickly become tame and learn to imitate words. Bare-eyed cockatoos have extremely loud voices and a strong need to gnaw.

Breeding: Although imported only in small numbers, breeding is often relatively successful. The largest breeding attempt up till now has been made by the San Diego (California) Zoo, which between 1929 and 1970 has produced 103 young from a single pair—most of which have been hand-raised. The clutch consists of 2 to 3 eggs. The length of brooding ranges from 21 to 24 days. The young leave the nest box after 45 to 50 days.

Greater Sulphur-crested Cockatoo

Cacatua galerita (4 subspecies)
[Photograph: page 9]

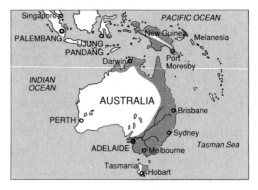

Description: Total length 19½ inches (50 cm). Male: basic plumage color white; ear spots—depending on subspecies—pale yellow to yellow; pointed crest, undersides of tail and wings yellow; unfeathered eye ring white; beak gray black; legs gray; iris deep dark brown to black. Female: similar to male, but iris is reddish brown. The triton cockatoo (*Cacatua galerita triton*) differs from all the other subspecies in that it has a blue, unfeathered eye ring.

Distribution: Northeastern and southern Australia, Tasmania, King Island, New Guinea, Aru Island.

Habitat: Open forested land, usually in the vicinity of water courses; occasionally also swampy areas and tropical rain forests.

Popular Cockatoo Species

Maintenance: After the Moluccan cockatoo, the greater sulphur-crested cockatoo is the largest representative of its species. It has an outstanding need to gnaw and utters piercing screams. Greater sulphur-crested cockatoos are not as a rule suited for apartment keeping. Young birds become very tame and have extraordinarily playful ways. Aviary birds are robust and undemanding. Except in the coldest of climates, they can even be wintered in unheated, but dry and draft-free, quarters.

Breeding: Often successful. Greater sulphur-crested cockatoos exhibit impressive courtship behavior, with fanned tail feathers, erected crests, and jerky display movements. The clutch consists of 2 to 3 eggs. The brooding time lasts around 30 days (both sexes take turns brooding, during the day by the male and night by the female). The nestling period lasts around 85 days. Young birds feed independently in about 100 days.

Lesser Sulphur-crested Cockatoo

Cacatua sulphurea (6 subspecies)
[Photographs: front cover, pages 27, 38]

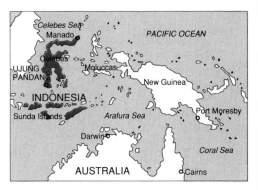

Description: Total length 13¼ inches (34 cm). Male: basic plumage color white; round ear spots, pointed crest, undersides of wings and tail yellow. Female: similar to male but iris turns brownish red after the third year. Of all six subspecies of the lesser sulphur-crested cockatoo, the citron-crested cockatoo (*Cacatua sulphurea citrinocristata*) is the most striking. Instead of the yellow markings it has orange ear spots and an orangey crest.

Distribution: Celebes (Sulawesi), Sunda Islands, several small islands of the Flores and the Java Seas.

Habitat: Open forest areas, occasionally unbroken forests and wheat-growing areas.

Maintenance: Most frequently kept in captivity of any of the cockatoo species; at one time they were particularly preferred as house pets, but today they are increasingly kept as pairs in the aviary. Lesser sulphur-crested cockatoos need roomy quarters, for they are good fliers; they are more active than the greater sulphur-crested. Their tremendous beak strength requires a sturdily built aviary. Natural branches and little boards should be provided regularly to prevent boredom and to satisfy their need to gnaw.

Breeding: Easiest to breed of all the cockatoos. Choosing mates does sometimes turn out to be somewhat difficult, however, for it can happen that the male will be very aggressive toward the female and chase her through the aviary, often to the point of exhaustion, and also drive her away from the feeding place. It is wise, therefore, to provide escape possibilities and blinders for the protection of the female. Sometimes it will be necessary to change mates. The courtship is very impressive, with erected crest, spread tail, erect strutting, and jerkey "bowing," similar to that of the greater sulphur-crested cockatoo. The clutch consists of 2 to 3 eggs, which are brooded by both sexes. Brooding lasts about 24 days (in citron-crested cockatoos 27 to 28 days). The nestling period takes between 8 and 10 weeks. Young do not acquire the black beak until they are approximately seven months old.

Umbrella-crested, White-crested, or Greater White-crested Cockatoo

Cacatua alba
[Photograph: page 38]

Popular Cockatoo Species

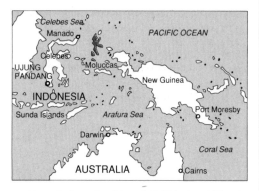

Description: Total length 17½ inches (45 cm). Male: basic plumage color white; broad-feathered crest white; unfeathered eye ring cream white; beak black; legs dark gray; iris dark brown to black. Female: similar to male, but iris red-brown.

Distribution: Moluccas Obi, Batjan, Soa-Siu (Tidore), and Ternate.

Habitat: Largely unknown; some authorities believe that the birds live in forests and around farmland in pairs or small groups.

Maintenance: Among the rarely kept species. The literature contains scarcely any reports about them. These parrots should be kept only in roomy, sturdy quarters, for they are very loud and their beaks are strong enough to destroy everything. Umbrella-crested cockatoos are not suitable for keeping in an apartment, although birds imported young are easily tamed and for a certain time can be trusted house pets. Aviary keeping is recommended, however; there the birds are relatively undemanding, but they do need a slightly warmed house for protection.

Breeding: The first successful breeding attempts were reported in the United States during the sixties and seventies; currently there are perhaps about ten breeding pairs in the German Federal Republic. The courtship probably starts with the female. Before copulation she performs a kind of courtship dance in which she hops from one leg to the other. The clutch consists of an average of 2 eggs. Brooding lasts from 29 to 30 days. The nestling period extends for 80 to 100 days.

Moluccan Cockatoo
Cacatua moluccensis
[Photograph: inside back cover]

Description: Total length 21½ inches (55 cm). Male: basic plumage color white, often with pinkish tinge; rounded crest with pink covert feathers and orange-red crest feathers; beak black; legs gray; iris black. Female: similar to male but iris deep brown.

Distribution: Molucca Islands Seram, Saparua, and Haruku, introduced to Ambon Island.

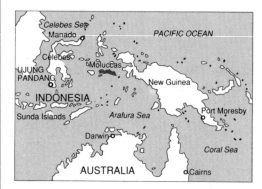

Habitat: Forested areas near the coast, principally low areas and hilly country under 3,280 feet (1000 m); in small flocks.

Maintenance: The largest cockatoos available commercially, they often are tamed ahead of time by the wholesaler. Their piercingly loud cries, destructive beak strength, and size, among other characteristics, make them utterly unsuitable for keeping in a cage in an apartment. Moluccan cockatoos are very sensitive animals and for a variety of reasons they are the most frequent feather pluckers of any of the parrots (see Illnesses, page 31). They are best maintained in pairs in an outdoor aviary of at least 6 feet (2m) wide and with plenty of opportunity for exercise and occupation. Some birds can even be kept on a climbing tree when their wing feathers are well clipped (see page 16).

Breeding: Only rarely succeeded; five or six successful attempts have been reported in the Republic of Germany in which chicks were reared by their parents. A number of Moluccan cockatoos have been hand-raised in Europe, England, and the United States. The sensitive nature of the bird, the difficulty in establishing a pair, the need for huge quarters, and the price of acquiring two birds considerably increase the difficulty of attempting to breed Moluccan cockatoos. The clutch usually consists of 2 to 3 eggs. The brooding period lasts 28 to 30 days. The nestling period extends for approximately 90 days.

Endangered and Extinct Species

Parrot Species in Danger of Extinction

Appendix I of the Washington Convention lists all the parrots that are in immediate danger of extinction or close to it. Trade in these birds is prohibited except for parrots that were raised in captivity. The most recent edition of Appendix I, drawn up at the fifth conference of May 1985, includes the following species.

Amazona arausiaca, red-necked Amazon
Amazona barabdensis, yellow-shouldered Amazon
Amazona brasiliensis, red-tailed Amazon
Amazona guildingii, St. Vincent Amazon
Amazona imperialis, imperial Amazon
Amazona leucocophala, Cuban Amazon
Amazona pretrei, red-spectacled Amazon
Amazon dufresniana rhodocorytha, red-crowned Amazon
Amazona versicolor, versicolor or St. Lucia Amazon
Amazona vinacea, vinaceous Amazon
Amazona vittata, Puerto Rican Amazon
Anadorhynchus glaucus, glaucus macaw (may be extinct)
Anadorhynchus leari, Lear's macaw
Ara rubrogenys, red-fronted or red-crowned macaw
Ara glaucogularis, blue-throated macaw
Ara ambigua, great green macaw
Ara macao, scarlet macaw
Ara militarias, military cockatoo
Aratinga guarouba, golden conure
Cyanopsitta spixii, Spix's macaw
Cyanoramphus auriceps forbesi, subspecies of yellow-fronted parakeet
Cyanoramphus novaezelandiae, red-fronted parakeet
Geopsittacus occidentalis, night parrot (may be extinct)
Neophema chrysogaster, orange-breasted parakeet
Ognorhynchus icterotis, yellow-eared conure
Opopsitta diophtalma coxeni, blue-browed or red-faced lorilet
Pezoporus wallicus, ground parakeet
Pionopsitta pileata, red-capped or pileated parrot
Probosciger aterrimus, great black cockatoo or palm cockatoo
Psephotus chrysopterygius, golden shouldered parakeet
Psephotus pulcherrimus, paradise parakeet (may be extinct)
Psittacula krameri echo, subspecies of Mauritius parakeet
Psittacus erithacus princeps, subspecies of gray parrot
Pyrrhura cruentata, red-eared conure
Rhynchopsitta spp., thick-billed parrots (two races)
Strigops habroptilus, owl parrot or kakapo

Extinct Species

A number of parrots became extinct during the eighteenth and nineteenth centuries. The reasons are not always known, but changes in and destruction of the parrots' natural habitat have been blamed as well as shooting of the birds for food and catching them for the pet trade. The following list contains all the species that are known to have existed, and in parentheses the date when they presumably died out is given.

Amazona vittata gracilipes, subspecies of Puerto Rican Amazon (1899)
Aratinga chloroptera maugei, Mauge's conure (ca. 1860)
Ara tricolor, Cuban macaw (1885)
Charmosyna diadema, New Caledonian lorikeet (ca. 1860)
Conuropsis carolinensis carolinensis, Carolina parakeet (ca. 1900)
Conuropsis carolinensis ludovicianus, subspecies of the above (1914)
Cyanoramphus novaezelandiae erythrotis, sub-

species of red-fronted parakeet (1800 to 1820)

Cyanoramphus novaezelandiae subflavescens, subspecies of red-fronted parakeet (ca. 1870)

Cyanoramphus ulietanus, society parakeet (1773/4)

Cyanoramphus zealandicus, black-fronted parakeet (1844)

Loriculus philippensis chrysonotus, subspecies of Philippines hanging parrot (after 1926)

Mascarinus mascarinus, Mascarene parrot (1800-1820)

Nestor meridionalis productus, Norfolk Island kaka (1851)

Psittacula eupatria wardi, Seychelles parakeet (ca. 1870)

Psittacula exsul, Newton's parakeet (ca. 1875)

Bringing Birds into the USA

What Is a Pet Bird?

A pet bird is defined as any bird, except poultry, intended for the personal pleasure of its individual owner, not for resale. Poultry, even if kept as pets, are imported under separate rules and quarantined at USDA animal import centers. Birds classified as poultry include chickens, turkeys, pheasants, partridge, ducks, geese, swans, doves, peafowl, and similar avian species.

Importing a Pet Bird

Special rules for bringing a pet bird into the United States (from all countries but Canada):

- USDA quarantine
- Quarantine space reservation
- Fee in advance
- Foreign health certificate
- Final shipping arrangements
- Two-bird limit

If you're bringing your pet bird into the country, you must

Quarantine your bird (or birds) for at least 30 days in a USDA-operated import facility at one of nine ports of entry. The bird, which must be caged when you bring it in, will be transferred to a special isolation cage at the import facility.

Reserve quarantine space for the bird. A bird without a reservation will be accepted only if space is available. If none exists, this bird either will be refused entry or be transported, at your expense, to another entry port where there is space.

Pay the USDA an advance fee of $40 to be applied to the cost of quarantine services and necessary tests and examinations. Currently, quarantine costs are expected to average $80 for one bird or $100 per isolation cage if more than one bird is put in a cage. These charges may change without notice. You may also have to pay private companies for brokerage and transportation services to move the bird from the port of entry to the USDA import facility.

Obtain a health certificate in the nation of the bird's origin. This is a certificate signed by a *national government* veterinarian stating that the bird has been examined, shows no evidence of communicable disease, and is being exported in accordance with the laws of that country. The certificate must be signed within 30 days of the time the birds arrive in the United States. If not in English, it must be translated at your cost.

Arrange for shipping the bird to its final destination when it is released from quarantine. A list of brokers for each of the nine ports of entry may be requested from USDA port veterinarians at the time quarantine space is reserved. (See addresses to follow.) Most brokers offer transportation services from entry port to final destination.

Bring no more than two psittacine birds (parrots, parakeets, and other hookbills) per family into the United States during any single year. Larger groups of these birds are imported under separate rules for commercial shipment of birds.

(Reprinted with permission from USDA-APHIS.)

Ports of Entry for Personally Owned Pet Birds

Listed below are the nine ports of entry for personally owned pet birds. To reserve quarantine space for your bird, write to the port veterinarian at the city where you'll be arriving and request Form 17-23. Return the completed form, together with a check or money order (contact the veterinarian in charge of the import facility for current costs) made payable to the USDA, to the same address. The balance of the fee will be due before the bird is released from quarantine.

Port Veterinarian

Bringing Birds into the USA

Animal and Plant Health Inspection Service
(APHIS)
U.S. Department of Agriculture
(City, State, Zip Code)
New York, New York 11430
Miami, Florida 33152
Laredo, Texas 78040
El Paso, Texas 79902
Nogales, Arizona 85621
San Ysidro, California 92073
Los Angeles, California (Mailing address,
Lawndale, CA 90261)
Honolulu, Hawaii 96850

The Quarantine Period

During quarantine, pet birds will be kept in individually controlled isolation cages to prevent any infection from spreading. Psittacine or hookbilled birds will be identified with a leg band. They will be fed a medicated feed as required by the U.S. Public Health Service to prevent psittacosis, a flulike disease transmissible to humans. Food and water will be readily available to the birds. Young, immature birds needing daily hand-feeding cannot be accepted because removing them from the isolation cage for feeding would interrupt the 30-day quarantine. During the quarantine, APHIS veterinarians will test the birds to make certain they are free of any communicable disease of poultry. Infected birds will be refused entry; at the owner's option they will either be returned to the country of origin (at the owner's expense) or humanely destroyed.

Special Exceptions

No government quarantine (and therefore no advance reservations or fees) and no foreign health certificate are required for:

• *U.S. birds taken out of the country if special arrangements are made in advance.* Before leaving the United States, you must get a health certificate for the bird from a veterinarian accredited by the USDA and make certain it is identified with a tattoo or numbered leg band. The health certificate, with this identification on it, must be presented at the time of re-entry. While out of the country, you must keep your pet bird separate from other birds. Remember that only two psittacine or hookbilled birds per family per year may enter the United States. Birds returning to the United States may come in through any one of the nine ports of entry listed earlier. There are also certain other specified ports of entry for these birds, depending upon the time of arrival and other factors. Contact APHIS officials for information on this prior to leaving the country.
• *Birds from Canada.* Pet birds may enter the United States from Canada on your signed statement that they have been in your possession for at least 90 days, were kept separate from other birds during the period, and are healthy. As with other countries, only two psittacine birds per family per year may enter the United States from Canada. Birds must be inspected by an APHIS veterinarian at designated ports of entry for land, air, and ocean shipments. These ports are subject to change, so for current information, contact APHIS/USDA officials.

Pet birds from Canada are not quarantined because Canada's animal disease control and eradication programs and import rules are similar to those of the United States.

Other U.S. Agencies Involved with Bird Imports

In addition to the U.S. Public Health Service requirement mentioned earlier, U.S. Department of the Interior rules require an inspection by one of its

Bringing Birds into the USA

officials to assure that an imported bird is not in the rare or endangered species category, is not an illegally imported migratory bird, and is not an agricultural pest or injurious to humans. For details from these agencies, contact:

Division of Law Enforcement,
Fish and Wildlife Service,
U.S. Department of the Interior,
Washington, D.C. 20240

Bureau of Epidemiology,
Quarantine Division,
Center for Disease Control,
U.S. Public Health Service,
Atlanta, Georgia 30333

U.S. Customs Service,
Department of the Treasury,
Washington, D.C. 20229
For additional information on USDA-APHIS regulations, contact,

Import-Export Staff,
Veterinary Services, APHIS,
U.S. Department of Agriculture,
Hyattsville, Maryland 20782.

Two Serious Threats to Birds

As a bird owner, you should know the symptoms of exotic *Newcastle disease*, the devastating disease of poultry and other birds mentioned elsewhere. If your birds show signs of incoordination and breathing difficulties—or if there should be any unusual die-off among them—contact your local veterinarian or animal health official immediately. Place dead birds in plastic bags, and refrigerate them for submittal to a diagnostic laboratory. Keep in mind that this disease is highly contagious, and you should isolate any newly purchased birds for at least 30 days. Although exotic Newcastle disease is not a general health hazard, it can cause minor eye infection in humans.

If you're tempted to buy a bird you suspect may have been smuggled into the United States, don't! Smuggled birds are a persistent threat to the health of pet birds and poultry flocks in this country. Indications are that many recent outbreaks of exotic Newcastle disease were caused by birds entering the United States illegally. If you have information about the possibility of smuggled birds, report it to any U.S. Customs office or call APHIS at Hyattsville, Maryland. (301) 436-8061.

Useful Literature and Addresses

Books

Birmelin, I. and Wolter, A. (1985). *The New Parakeet Handbook*, Barron's Educational Series, Hauppauge, New York.

Cayley N.W., and Lendon, A. (1973). *Australian Parrots in Field and Aviary*, Angus & Robertson, Sydney, Australia.

Diemer, P. (1983). *Parrots*, Barron's Educational Series, Hauppauge, New York.

Eastman, W.R., and Hunt, A. C. (1966). *The Parrots of Australia*, Angus & Robertson, Sydney, Australia.

Forshaw, J.M. (1981). *Australian Parrots*, 2nd edition, Lansdowne Press, Melbourne, Australia.

—(1978). *Parrots of the World*, 2nd edition, Lansdowne Press, Melbourne, Australia.

Harman, I. (1981). *Australian Parrots in Bush and Aviary*, Inkata Press, Melbourne and Sydney, Australia.

Lantermann, W. (1986). *The New Parrot Handbook*, Barron's Educational Series, Hauppauge, New York.

Low, R. (1989). *The Complete Book of Parrots*, Barron's Educational Series, Hauppauge, New York.

—(1984). *Endangered Parrots*, Blandford Press, Poole, Dorset, England.

—(1980). *Parrots, Their Care and Breeding*, Blandford Press, Poole, Dorset, England.

Moizer, S. and B. (1988). *The Complete Book of Budgerigars*, Barron's Educational Series, Hauppauge, New York.

Petrak, M.L. (1982). *Diseases of Cage and Aviary Birds*, 2nd edition, Lea & Febiger, Philadelphia.

Ruthers, A., and Norris, K.A. (1972). *Encyclopedia of Aviculture*, Vol. 2, Blandford Press, Poole, Dorset, England.

Vriends, M. M. (1986). *Lovebirds*, Barron's Educational Series, Hauppauge, New York.

—(1986). *Simon and Schuster's Guide to Pet Birds*, Simon and Schuster, New York.

—(1987). *The Macdonald Encyclopedia of Cage and Aviary Birds*, Macdonald & Co., Publishers, Ltd., London and Sydney, Australia.

—(1989). *The New Bird Handbook,* Barron's Educational Series, Hauppauge, New York.

Wolter, A., (1987). *African Gray Parrots*,Barron's Educational Series, Hauppauge, New York.

Periodicals

American Cage Bird Magazine (Monthly; One Glamore Court, Smithtown, New York 11787)

Avicultural Bulletin (Monthly; Avicultural Society of America, Inc., P.O. Box 2796, Dept. CB, Redondo Beach, CA 90278)

Avicultural Magazine (Quarterly; The Avicultural Society, Windsor, Forest Stud, Mill Ride, Ascot, Berkshire, England)

Cage and Aviary Birds (Weekly; Prospect House, 9-15 Ewell Road, Cheam, Sutton, Surrey, SM3 8BZ, England); young birdkeepers under 16 may like to join the *Junior Bird League*; full details can be obtained from the J.B.L.,*c/o Cage and Aviary Birds*

Magazine of the Parrot Society (Monthly; 19a De Parys Ave., Bedford, Bedfordshire, England)

Parrotworld (Monthly; National Parrot Association, 8 North Hoffman Lane, Hauppauge, New York 11788)

Watchbird (Bi-monthly; American Federation of Aviculture, P.O. Box 1568, Redondo Beach, CA 90278)

American Bird Clubs

Avicultural Society of America (see *Avicultural Bulletin*)

American Federation of Aviculture, Inc. (see *The A.F.A. Watchbird*)

National Parrot Association (see *Parrotworld*)

Australian Bird Clubs

Avicultural Society of Australia, c/o Mr. I.C.L. Jackson, Box 130, Broadford, Victoria 3658

Avicultural Society of Queensland, 19 Fahey's

Useful Literature and Addresses

Road, Albany Creek, Queensland, 4035

Canadian Bird Clubs

Avicultural Advancement Council, P.O. Box 5126, Postal Station "B," Victoria, British Columbia, V8R 6N4

British Columbia Avicultural Society, c/o Mr. Paul Prior, 11784-90th Avenue, North Delta, British Columbia, V4C 3H6

Calgary and District Avicultural Society, c/o Mr. Richard Kary, 7728 Bowcliffe Cr., N.W. Calgary, Alberta, T3B 2S5

Canadian Parrot Association, Pine Oaks, R.R. Nr. 3, St. Catherines, Ontario, L2R 6P9

English Bird Clubs

The Avicultural Society (see *Avicultural Magazine*)

The Parrot Society (see *Magazine of the Parrot Society*)

New Zealand Bird Club

The Avicultural Society of New Zealand Inc., P.O. Box 21403, Henderson, Auckland 8

Veterinarian Association

Association of Avian Veterinarians, P.O. Box 299, East Northport, New York 11731

Index

Page numbers in *italics* indicate color photos. *C2* indicates inside front cover; *C3*, inside back cover; *C4*, back cover.

Index

Index

Perfect for Pet Owners!